Just for the Lower Le...

- Test Prep Works materials are developed for a specific test and level, making it easier for students to focus on relevant content

- The Lower Level ISEE is for students applying for admission to grades 5-6 – see table at the end of this book for materials for other grades

- Three books are available from Test Prep Works to help students prepare for the Lower Level ISEE

Success on the Lower Level ISEE: A Complete Course

- Strategies for each section of the test
- Reading and vocabulary drills
- In-depth math content instruction with practice sets
- 1 full-length practice test

30 Days to Acing the Lower Level ISEE

- Strategies for each section of the test
- Fifteen "workouts", each providing practice problems and detailed explanations for every section of the test
- Perfect for additional practice or homework

The Best Unofficial Practice Tests for the Lower Level ISEE

- 2 additional full-length practice tests

TEST PREP WORKS, LLC.

Are you an educator?

Incorporate materials from Test Prep Works into your test prep program

- Use the materials developed specifically for the test and level your students are taking

- Customize our books to fit your program

    - Choose content modules from any of our books — even from multiple books

    - Add your branding to the cover and title page

    - Greet your students with an introductory message

    - Create custom books with a one-time setup fee[1], then order copies at list price[2] with no minimum quantities

- Volume discounts available for bulk orders of 50+ copies

You provide the expertise — let us provide the materials

Contact *sales@testprepworks.com* for more info

1 - Setup fees start at $199 per title, which includes branding of the cover and title page and a customer-provided introductory message. Additional customization will incur additional setup fees.

2 - The list price for custom books is the same as the list price of the corresponding title available for retail sale. If the content of a book is modified so that it no longer corresponds to a book available for retail sale, then Test Prep Works will set the list price prior to assessing any setup fees.

TEST PREP WORKS, LLC.

30 DAYS

TO *Acing* THE

Lower Level ISEE

Strategies and Practice for Maximizing Your Lower Level ISEE Score

Christa Abbott, M.Ed.

Copyright © 2014 Test Prep Works, LLC. All rights reserved. Except as permitted under the Copyright Act of 1976, no part of this publication may be reproduced or distributed in any forms or by any means, or stored in a data base or retrieval system, without the prior written permission of the publisher.

Published by:
Test Prep Works, LLC
PO Box 100572
Arlington, VA 22210
www.TestPrepWorks.com

For information about buying this title in bulk, or for editions with customized covers or content, please contact us at sales@testprepworks.com or (703) 944-6727.

ISEE is a registered trademark of the ERB. They have not endorsed nor are they associated with this book.

Neither the author nor the publisher of this book claims responsibility for the accuracy of this book or the outcome of students who use these materials.

ISBN: 978-1-939090-12-6

Contents

About the Author

Christa Abbott has been a private test prep tutor for over a decade. She has worked with students who have been admitted to and attended some of the top independent schools in the country. Over the years, she has developed materials for each test that truly make the difference.

Christa is a graduate of Middlebury College and received her Masters in Education from the University of Virginia, a program nationally known for its excellence. Her background in education allows her to develop materials based on the latest research about how we learn so that preparation can be an effective and efficient use of time. Her materials are also designed to be developmentally appropriate for the ages of the students taking the tests. In her free time, she enjoys hiking, tennis, Scrabble, and reading. Her greatest joy is spending time with her husband and three children.

Christa continues to work with students one-on-one in the Washington, D.C., area. She also works with students internationally via Skype. If you are interested in these services, please visit www.ChristaAbbott.com.

About Test Prep Works, LLC

Test Prep Works, LLC, was founded to provide effective materials for test preparation. Its founder, Christa Abbott, spent years looking for effective materials for the private school entrance exams but came up empty-handed. The books available combined several different tests and while there are overlaps, they are not the same test. Christa found this to be very overwhelming for students who were in elementary and middle school and that just didn't seem necessary. Christa developed her own materials to use with students that are specific for each level of the test and are not just adapted from other books. For the first time, these materials are available to the general public as well as other tutors. Please visit www.TestPrepWorks.com to view a complete array of offerings as well as sign up for a newsletter with recent news and developments in the world of admissions and test preparation.

How to Use This Book

This book is designed to teach you what you need to know in order to maximize your Lower Level ISEE performance. The book starts with a brief introduction to strategies for each section. After that, there is a series of "workouts". Each of these workouts should take about 30 minutes.

Within each workout, I have included strategy and practice for each section so that you get a "balanced diet" leading up to test day. You will notice some repetition – this is by design! In particular, you may see vocabulary words or words with the same roots repeated. This is to ensure that you don't forget the vocabulary that you have already studied. After you complete each workout, be sure to check your answers and figure out WHY you missed the questions that you did. The analysis is as important as the answers themselves.

I have spent years studying the test and analyzing the different question types, content, and the types of answers that test writers prefer. Now you can benefit from my hard work! First work through the strategy sections at the beginning of the book. The workouts will then reinforce these strategies as well as expose you to new vocabulary and content.

Let's get started!

P.S. In this book, we want to focus on the strategies and not go into the nitty-gritty of how to register and test details. All of this information is available at:

http://www.erblearn.org/parents/admission/isee

If you click on "Preparing for the ISEE" link on this page you can also download a practice test from the actual writers of the test (it is contained in the "What to Expect on the ISEE" book).

The 30 Days to ISEE Success Game Plan

Step 1: Read through the strategies section of this book.

Take the time to really understand each strategy, but know that what you have learned will be reinforced in the workouts.

Step 2: Complete the workouts.

When you miss a question, take the time to understand WHY you missed it before you move on to the next workout. Make flashcards for words or roots that you don't know and study them as you go.

Step 3: Read the appendix.

It gives advice on how to tackle the writing sample.

Step 4: Take the practice test.

Download "What to Expect on the ISEE" from http://www.erblearn.org/parents/admission/isee. This includes a practice test from the actual test writers – an invaluable resource.

Step 5: Rock the ISEE!

If you are looking for additional Lower Level ISEE resources such as additional practice tests or content instruction, please visit www.testprepworks.com for more information on our other materials for the Lower Level ISEE.

What You Need to Know for the ISEE – Just the Basics

How the scoring works

On the ISEE, your score is determined just by how many questions you answer correctly. They do not take off any points if you answer a question incorrectly.

When to guess

On the ISEE, you want to answer absolutely everything, even if you haven't looked at the question. You may answer the question correctly, and they don't take off any points for questions that you answer incorrectly. If you are running out of time or don't understand a question, just blindly guess – you may choose the right answer!

The percentile score

You will get a raw score for the ISEE based upon how many questions you answer correctly. This raw score will then be converted into a scaled score. Neither of these scores is what schools are really looking at. They are looking for your percentile scores.

- Percentile score is what schools are really looking at

The percentile score compares you to other students that are in your grade. For example, let's say that you are an eighth grader and you scored in the 70th percentile. What this means is that out of a hundred students in your grade, you would have done better than 70 of them.

- Your percentile score compares you only to other students in your grade

Many students applying to independent schools are used to getting almost all the questions correct on a test. You will probably miss more questions on this test than you are used to missing, but because the percentile score is what schools are looking at, don't let it get to you.

- You may miss more questions than you are used to, but that is OK as long as other students your age miss those questions

You should look at the scoring charts in "What to Expect on the ISEE" (downloaded from erblearn.org). These charts will give you a rough idea of how many questions you need to answer correctly in order to achieve different percentile scores.

Students always want to know, "What is a good percentile score?" Well, that depends on the schools you are applying to. The best resources are the admissions officers at the schools that you want to attend.

The Format of the Lower Level ISEE

You can expect to see four scored sections plus an essay. The sections are listed below in the order that they will appear on the ISEE. One great thing about the ISEE is that it has a very predictable format.

The four scored sections

- Verbal Reasoning
  - ✓ 17 vocabulary questions
  - ✓ 17 sentence completion questions
- Quantitative Reasoning
  - ✓ 38 math word problems
  - ✓ Less focused on calculations and equations, more focused on thinking through a problem
- Reading Comprehension
  - ✓ 25 total questions
  - ✓ 5 passages, each with 5 questions about it
- Mathematics Achievement
  - ✓ 30 math questions
  - ✓ More focused on calculations and knowing specific math terminology than the quantitative reasoning section

The essay

- Prompt for students to respond to
- 30 minutes to complete
- Two lined pieces of paper to write response on
- NOT scored, but a copy of the essay is sent to schools that student applies to

Now, on to the strategies and content! The strategies covered in this book will focus on the multiple-choice sections since those are what is used to determine your score. Please also see the appendix for tips on how to write the essay.

-

The Mother of All Strategies

Use the process of elimination, or "ruling out"

If you remember nothing else on test day, remember to use the process of elimination. This is a multiple-choice test, and there are often answers that don't even make sense.

When you read a question, you want to read all of the answer choices before selecting one. You need to keep in mind that the test will ask you to choose the answer choice that "best" answers the question. Best is a relative word, so how can you know which answer choice best answers the question if you don't read them all?

- After you read the question, read ALL of the answer choices
- Look for the "best" answer, which may be the least wrong answer choice

After you have read all of the answer choices, rule them out in order from most wrong to least wrong. Sometimes the "best" answer choice is not a great fit, but it is better than the others. This process will also clarify your thinking so that by the time you get down to only two answer choices, you have a better idea of what makes choices right or wrong.

- Rule out in order from most wrong to least wrong

On the ISEE, they don't take off for wrong answer choices, so it can be tempting to just blindly guess if you are confused. However, put a little of work into the question before you do that. Even if you are having trouble understanding a question, there may be one or two answer choices that don't even make sense.

- Use ruling out before you guess, even if the question leaves you totally confused

Verbal Reasoning – Basic Strategies

In the verbal section you will see two question types:

- Synonyms
- Sentence completions

On the synonym questions, you will be given one question word and then you have to choose the answer choice that has the word that comes closest in meaning to that question word.

Synonym questions look something like this:

1. JOYOUS:

    (A) crying
    (B) happy
    (C) loud
    (D) mad

Out of all the answer choice words, *happy* comes closest in meaning to *joyous*. Choice B is correct.

The synonym questions won't all be that easy, but you get the idea.

The sentence completion questions give you a sentence with a dashed line that has replaced one or more words. Your job is to figure out which answer choice should be inserted instead of that dashed line so that the sentence makes sense.

The sentence completion questions usually look something like this:

2. The student was afraid that she had not done well on the test, but when she got her scores back she was pleasantly -------.

    (A) boisterous
    (B) panicked
    (C) surprised
    (D) worried

In this case, the beginning of the sentence tells us that the student thinks she hasn't done well. We then have the conjunction "but" which tells us that the second part of the sentence will contradict the first, so something good must have happened. Choice C fits the bill and it is the correct answer choice.

There are also sentence completion questions that ask us to choose which phrase would best complete the sentence rather than just a word. The key to these questions is to stick to the main idea of the half of the sentence that we are given.

Here is an example of this type of question:

3. At top of the roller coaster, the children -------.

    (A) went to their next class
    (B) got dressed for the day
    (C) squealed with delight
    (D) finished their lunches

What is the first part of the sentence talking about? It is talking about being at the top of a roller coaster. Would it make sense to go to a class, get dressed for the day, or finish your lunch at the top of a roller coaster? No. But it would make sense to squeal with delight. Answer choice C is correct.

These are the basic question types that you will see in the Verbal Reasoning section. They are very different, so we have different strategies for each question type.

Synonyms strategies

There are several strategies that we can use on the synonyms section. Which strategy you use for an individual question is up to you. It depends on what roots you know, whether or not you have heard the word before, and your gut sense about a word.

Think of these strategies as being your toolbox. Several tools can get the job done.

Here are the strategies:

- Come up with your own word
- Use positive or negative
- Use context
- Look for roots or word parts that you know

Strategy #1: Come up with your own word

Use this strategy when you read through a sentence and a word just pops into your head. Don't force yourself to try to come up with your own definition when you aren't sure what the word means.

- Use this strategy when the definition pops into your head

If you read a question word and a synonym pops into your head, go ahead and jot it down. It is important that you write down the word because otherwise you may try to talk yourself into an answer choice that "seems to come close". One of the biggest enemies on any standardized test is doubt. Doubt leads to talking yourself into the wrong answer choice, and physically writing down the word gives you the confidence you need when you go through the answer choices.

- Physically write down the definition – don't hold it in your head

After you write down the word, start by crossing out answer choices that are not synonyms for your word. By the time you get down to two choices, you will have a much better idea of what you are looking for.

- Cross out words that don't work

Here are a couple of examples for you to try:

1. RAPID:

    (A) exhausted
    (B) marvelous
    (C) professional
    (D) swift

2. DAINTY:

    (A) delicate
    (B) long
    (C) surprising
    (D) warm

Answers:

1. In order to use this strategy, we would jot down a word next to *rapid*. Maybe we would write down "fast" or "quick". Since the word *swift* comes closest to these words, answer choice D is correct.

2. Next to the word *dainty*, we might write down "small" or "fragile". Since *delicate* comes closest in meaning to these words, answer choice A is correct.

Strategy #2: Use positive or negative

Sometimes you see a word, and you couldn't define that word, but you have a "gut feeling" that it is either something good or something bad. Maybe you don't know what that word means, but you know you would be mad if someone called you that!

- You have to have a "gut feeling" about a word to use this strategy

To use this strategy, when you get that feeling that a word is either positive or negative, write a "+" or a "–" sign next to the word. Then go to your answer choices and rule out anything that is opposite, i.e., positive when your question word is negative or negative when your question word is positive.

- Physically write a "+" or "–" sign after the question word
- Rule out words that are opposite

To really make this strategy work for you, you also need to rule out any words that are neutral, or neither positive nor negative. For example, let's say the question word is DISTRESS. *Distress* is clearly a negative word. So we could rule out a positive answer choice, such as *friendly*, but we can also rule out a neutral word, such as *sleepy*. At night, it is good to be sleepy, during the day it is not. *Sleepy* is not clearly a negative word, so it goes.

- Rule out neutral words

To summarize, here are the basic steps to using this strategy:

1. If you have a gut negative or positive feeling about a word, write a "+" or "–" sign next to the question word.
2. Rule out any words that are opposite.
3. Also rule out any NEUTRAL words.
4. Pick from what is left.

Here are a couple of examples where you may be able to use the positive/negative strategy:

1. CONDEMN:

   (A) arrive
   (B) blame
   (C) favor
   (D) tint

2. HUMANE:

   (A) compassionate
   (B) invalid
   (C) portable
   (D) restricted

Answers:

1. Let's say that you know that *condemn* is bad, but you don't know the definition. We write a "–" sign next to it and then rule out any positive words. Choice C can go because it is positive. We can also rule out neutral words because *condemn* is negative. *Arrive* and *tint* are neither positive nor negative, so choices A and D are out. We are left with choice B, which is correct.

2. Maybe you have heard of a "humane society" before that takes care of animals that do not have homes. That sounds positive, right? So we put a "+" sign next to the word *humane*. We can rule out *invalid* and *restricted* because these are negative words. We can also eliminate *portable* because it means "able to be carried" which is a neutral word. We are left with choice A, which is the correct answer.

Strategy #3: Use context – Think of where you have heard the word before

Use this strategy when you can't define a word, but you can think of a sentence or phrase in which you have heard the word before.

- This strategy only works when you have heard the word before

To apply this strategy, think of a sentence or phrase you have heard before with the question word. Then try plugging the answer choices into your phrase to see which one has the same meaning within that sentence or phrase.

- Think of where you have heard the word before
- Plug question words into that sentence or phrase

Here are a couple of examples of questions that you might be able to use this strategy for:

1. ENDORSE:

   (A) drain
   (B) import
   (C) prowl
   (D) support

2. BRAWNY:

   (A) awake
   (B) coarse
   (C) strong
   (D) tiny

Answers:

1. Let's say that you can't think of a definition for the word *endorse*, but you have heard people say that they "endorse a candidate" for political office. Now we plug our answer choices into that phrase and see what would have the same meaning. Would it make sense to "drain a candidate"? Nope. Answer choice A is out. Would it make sense to "import a candidate" or "prowl a candidate"? No and no. Answer choices B and C are out. Finally, would it make sense to say that you "support a candidate"? Absolutely. Answer choice D is correct.

2. Have you heard of Brawny paper towels before? That name was chosen for a reason. Would a company want people to associate *awake*, *coarse*, *strong*, or *tiny* with their paper towels? Customers would want strong paper towels. Answer choice C is correct.

Strategy #4: Look for roots or word parts that you know

This strategy works when you recognize that a word looks like another word that you know or when you recognize one of the roots that you have studied in school or in this book.

If you see something familiar in the question word, underline the roots or word parts that you recognize. If you can think of the meaning of the root, then look for answer choices that would go with that meaning. If you can't think of a specific meaning, think of other words that have that root and look for answer choices that are similar in meaning to those other words.

- Underline word parts that you recognize
- Think of the meaning of that word part
- If you don't know the meaning of that word part, think of other words with that same word part

Here are a couple of examples of questions that use a word with recognizable word parts:

1. EXCLUDE:

    (A) drift
    (B) find
    (C) prohibit
    (D) send

2. SUBTERRANEAN:

   (A) faded
   (B) partial
   (C) tragic
   (D) underground

Answers:

1. There are two word parts in the word *exclude* that can help us out. First, we have the prefix *ex*, which means "out" (think of the word *exit*). Secondly, *clu* is a word root that means "to shut" (think of the word *include*). Using these word parts, we can see that *exclude* has something to do with shutting out. Choice C comes closest to this meaning, so it is correct.

2. In the word *subterranean* we have two word parts. The root *sub* means "under" and the root *terra* means "earth" or "ground". These roots tell us that *underground*, or choice D, is the correct answer.

Sentence Completions strategies

We have several strategies in our toolbox for sentence completion questions.

They include:

- Underline the key idea
- Look for sentences showing contrast
- Look for sentences showing cause or sequence
- Use our strategies for synonyms when you don't know the meaning of one or more of the answer choices

Strategy #1: Underline the key idea

Perhaps our most powerful strategy is to underline what the sentence is about.

If you are unsure of what to underline, look for the part of the sentence that if you changed that word or phrase, you would change what you were looking for.

- Look for the part of the sentence that if you changed it, you would change what word or phrase would fit in the blank
- Underline this key word or phrase

After you underline the key word or phrase, try coming up with your own word or phrase that would fit in the blank. This will help you easily rule out answer choices that are not like your word.

- After you underline the key word/phrase, fill in your own word or phrase in the blank

Here is an example:

1. The artist spent his days ------ the walls in the cave.

2. The scientist spent his days ------ the walls in the cave.

Do you see how changing just one word changed what we would put in that blank? If the person was an artist, we might expect him to be painting the walls in the cave. If the person was a scientist, however, we would expect him to maybe be studying the walls in the cave or analyzing the walls in the cave.

Here are a couple of examples for you to try – remember to underline the key word:

1. Author Charles Dickens ------ class structure in Victorian London.

   (A) describes
   (B) ignores
   (C) limits
   (D) paints

2. The path seemed to wander in a ----- manner, twisting and turning through the woods.

   (A) paved
   (B) obedient
   (C) roundabout
   (D) straight

Answers:

1. For this question, we would underline *author* as the key word. What do authors do? They describe. Choice A is correct.

2. In this question, we would underline *twisting and turning*. This tells us that we want a word that comes close in meaning to *twisting and turning* and answer choice C comes closest.

Strategy #2: Look for sentences showing contrast

Some sentences show contrast. With these sentences, the end of the sentence changes direction from the beginning of the sentence.

These sentences often use the words "but", "although", "however", "rather", and "even though". If you see any of these words, circle them.

The first step in answering these questions is to underline the key word or phrase. We need to know what we are contrasting with. The next step is to circle the words that show contrast, such as "but", "although", "however", "rather", and "even though".

- Underline key word or phrase
- Circle word(s) that show contrast such as "but", "although", "however", "rather", and "even though"

Here are a couple of examples:

1. Although the student tried to stay interested, her expression clearly showed that she was -------.

   (A) bored
   (B) jealous
   (C) mysterious
   (D) positive

2. Although Sarah was usually on time for work, when it snowed -------.

(A) she could not avoid being late for work
(B) she wore a colorful scarf and earmuffs to work
(C) she was cold all day long
(D) she booked a vacation in the tropics

Answers:

1. In this question, we circle the word *although* since it shows contrast. Then we underline the word *interested* since the sentence is about the student staying interested (if we changed that word, we would change what the blank would be). Since we have the word *although* we know that we are looking for a word that contrasts with *interested*. Since *bored* is the opposite of *interested*, choice A is correct.

2. The trick to this question is to pay close attention to the beginning of the sentence. The beginning of the sentence talks about how Sarah is usually on time for work. It also has the word *although* so we know that we are looking for something that is the opposite of being on time for work. Only choice A contrasts with being on time for work, so it is the correct answer. For this question it would be really easy to focus on the fact that it is snowing. If we were just paying attention to the snow, then choices B, C, and D would be possibilities. To avoid falling for this trap, go back to the basics. Underline the key word or phrase in the beginning of the sentence and stick to that.

Strategy #3: Look for sentences showing cause or sequence

Many sentences in the sentence completions section use the cause or sequence relationship. In these sentences, one thing leads to another. Sometimes one directly causes the other, but sometimes one just happens to come after the other.

- Look for sentences where one thing leads to another
- Think about what the effect of the given action would be

Sometimes you will see the words "because", "when", or "after" in these sentences, but there is often no one particular word that indicates cause.

- If you see the words "because", "when", "after", or other words showing sequence, you usually have a sentence showing cause or sequence

Here are a couple of examples:

1. Years of floods and fires left the former resort ------.

    (A) busy
    (B) effective
    (C) patriotic
    (D) wrecked

2. Since the dance team won a large cash prize, they ------.

    (A) changed their performance
    (B) came up with a new name
    (C) could afford to travel to another competition
    (D) dissolved the team

Answers:

1. To answer this question, we have to ask ourselves what years of floods and fires would lead to. While you could say that the resort would be left *busy* because they had lot of cleanup work to do, the more direct answer would be that it was left *wrecked*. Choice D is the correct answer.

2. For this question, we have to remember to look for the answer that could most directly be caused by the team winning a large cash prize. Answer choices A, B, and D could be caused by winning a cash prize in some roundabout way. However, more money could directly lead to the team being able to afford another competition. Answer choice C is correct.

Strategy #4: Use our strategies for synonyms when you don't know the meaning of one or more of the answer choices

Sometimes you know what kind of word you are looking for, but the problem is that you don't know the meaning of some of the answer choices. If this is the case, ask yourself:

*   Am I looking for a positive or negative word?
*   Do any of the answer choices have roots or prefixes that I can use?
*   Have I heard any of the answer choices used in a sentence or phrase before?

Reading Comprehension – Basic Strategies

On the reading comprehension section you will be given five passages, each with five questions about it. The reading section is very predictable!

Follow the basic plan below. Don't worry, you will get plenty of chances to practice your strategies with the passages in the workouts.

Reading section plan of attack

Students can significantly improve their reading scores by following an easy plan:

Step 1: Plan your time.
You have five minutes per passage, so be sure to lay out your time before you begin. You can make a basic chart showing the start time and then when you should finish the first passage (five minutes after the start), when you should finish the second passage (five minutes after you finish the first passage), and so on.

Step 2: Prioritize passages.
Play to your strengths. Don't just answer the passages in the order that they appear. Look for shorter passages. Also, think about whether you are better at fiction or nonfiction passages.

Step 3: Go to the questions first.
Mark questions as either specific or general. If the question is specific, underline what the question is asking about. You want to know what to look for as you read.

Step 4: Read the passage.
If you run across the answer to a specific question, go ahead and answer that. But do not worry if you miss an answer. The goal here is just to get a sense of where information is in the passage.

Step 5: Answer specific questions.
If there are any specific questions that you did not answer yet, go back and find the answers. For specific questions, you should be able to underline the correct answer restated in the passage.

Step 6: Answer general questions.

Answer any questions that ask about the passage as a whole. Before answering general questions, reread the last sentence of the entire passage. This will help you figure out the main idea of the passage.

Step 7: Repeat steps 3-6 with next passage.

You've got it under control. Keep cranking through the section until you are done.

Keep in mind that this section is not a test of how well you read. It is a test of how well you test. You need to manage your time and think about the process.

So how do we know if a question is specific or general?

It is important that you mark questions as specific (S) or general (G). You may come across the answer to a specific questions are you read, so you also want to underline what the question is asking about for specific questions.

A specific question asks for a detail from a small part of the passage. Here are some examples of specific questions:

- In line 15, the word "escape" most nearly means
- What can be inferred from the first sentence (lines 1-3)?
- According to the author, the totem pole was used for
- Which of the following questions can be answered with information from the passage?

If there is a line number or the question asks about a detail that is not the main idea, then we know it has to be a specific question.

A general question asks about the passage as a whole. Here are some examples of general questions:

- The main purpose of this passage is to
- This passage is primarily concerned with
- The author's tone is
- Which word best characterizes how bees are described in the passage?

Secrets for choosing the correct answer

Secret #1: On specific questions, watch out for answer choices that have words from the passage

On the ISEE, answer choices often have words from the passage, but they might insert another word or two so that the meaning is different. Some answer choices also have words from the passage, but they are not the correct answer to that particular question.

- Be cautious when choosing an answer that repeats words from the passage

Here is an example. Let's say that the passage states:

John was upset when Sam got into the car with Trish.

The question may look something like:

1. Which of the following is implied by the author?

   (A) John was upset with Trish when he got into the car.
   (B) Sam and Trish were upset when John got into the car.
   (C) John and Sam were cousins.
   (D) John was not happy when Sam rode with Trish.

Answer choices A and B use words from the passage, but do not have the same meaning as what the passage says. Choice C is unrelated – which happens on the ISEE! Choice D restates what the passage says.

Secret #2: On general questions, be sure not to pick an answer that is a detail

The test writers need students to miss general questions. Generally, if a student sees an answer choice that was mentioned in the passage, this answer choice will be really tempting! These answer choices are wrong, however, because they are details and not the main idea. The best way to focus in on the real main idea is to reread the last sentence before answering a general question.

- Look out for answers that are details – these are the wrong answers for main idea questions
- Reread the last sentence before answering a general question

Quantitative Reasoning and Mathematics Achievement – Basic Strategies

On the quantitative sections, there are problems from arithmetic, algebra, and geometry as well as questions that ask you to interpret data and probabilities. The math is really not that hard. The ISEE is more about applying what you have learned than answering complicated questions.

You will NOT be allowed to use a calculator on the ISEE. By using strategies, however, we can get to the right answers, often without using complicated calculations.

- No calculator allowed

The goal here is for you to get a general understanding of the key strategies for the math sections.

Drumroll, please! The strategies are:

- Estimate – this is a multiple-choice test!
- If there are variables in the answer choices, try plugging in your own numbers
- If they ask for the value of a variable, plug in answer choices

Strategy #1: Estimate

You can spend a lot of time finding the exact right answer on this test, or you can spend time figuring out what answers couldn't possibly work and then choose from what is left.

For example, let's say the question is:

1. Use the pictures below to answer the question.

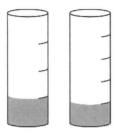

The pictures above show two jars that each hold 1 liter of liquid when they are full. They are not currently full (as shown). If the liquid from the two jars was combined, about how many liters of liquid would there be in total?

(A) $\dfrac{9}{20}$

(B) $1\dfrac{1}{5}$

(C) $1\dfrac{1}{2}$

(D) $2\dfrac{1}{4}$

We could read each jar and see that one jar has $\dfrac{1}{4}$ of a liter in it and the other jar has $\dfrac{1}{5}$ of a liter in it and then add those fractions together. However, we don't need to do that! We can clearly see that each jar is less than half full. That means that the total volume of the two combined would have to be less than a liter. Only answer choice A is less than a liter, so we can answer the question correctly without doing involved calculations.

You can use estimation on many of the problems, but in particular estimate when the question tells you to! You may see questions that ask for a "reasonable estimate" and then give answer choices in a range. Definitely estimate on those questions.

Here is an example:

2. Sean buys four items at the store that cost $3.21, $4.83, $6.05, and $2.99. What would be a reasonable estimate for the total cost of his items?

    (A) between $12 and $15
    (B) between $15 and $19
    (C) between $19 and $25
    (D) between $25 and $30

Without a calculator, finding the exact sum of the prices of the items would be kind of a bummer. However, the answer choices are just looking for a range, so we can round off. We would round off the prices to $3, $5, $6, and $3. If we add these numbers up, we get a total of $17. That clearly falls between $15 and $19, so answer choice B is correct.

Another way to use estimates is to come up with a range that the answer should fall within. You might find that the answer choices are spread far enough apart that only one answer choice falls within your range. This is particularly helpful for subtraction problems with big numbers or problems that require subtracting fractions.

Here is an example where we can find a range:

3. Which is equal to the difference $3,000 - 245$?

    (A) 2,555
    (B) 2,655
    (C) 2,755
    (D) 2,855

The first step to finding a range is to find a range for the number that is being subtracted. The number 245 is between 200 and 300. We subtract each of these numbers from 3,000 to get a range that the correct answer must fall in between.

$3,000 - 200 = 2,800$
$3,000 - 300 = 2,700$

We can see that the correct answer must be between 2,700 and 2,800. Only answer choice C falls between 2,700 and 2,800, so it is the correct answer.

Strategy #2: Plug in your own numbers if there are variables in the answer choices

What do I mean by variables in the answer choices? If you look at the answer choices and some or all of them have letters in addition to numbers, then you have variables in your answer choices.

- Look for letters in the answer choices

Here is how this strategy works:

1. Make up your own numbers for the variables.

   Just make sure they work within the problem. If they say that x is less than 1, do not make x equal to 2! If they say $x + y = 1$, then for heaven's sake, don't make x equal to 2 and y equal to 3. Also, make sure that you write down what you are plugging in for your variables. EVERY TIME.

2. Solve the problem using your numbers.

   Write down the number that you get and circle it. This is the number you are trying to get with your answer choices when you plug in your value for the variable.

3. Plug the numbers that you assigned to the variables in step 1 into the answer choices and see which answer choice matches the number that you circled.

Here is an example:

1. Suzy has q more pencils than Jim. If Jim has 23 pencils, then how many pencils does Suzy have?

   (A) $\dfrac{q}{23}$

   (B) $q - 23$

   (C) $q + 23$

   (D) $23 - q$

Step 1: Plug in our own number.

Let's make q equal to 4. Suzy now has 4 more pencils than Jim.

Step 2: Solve using our own numbers.

If Jim has 23 pencils, and Suzy has four more than Jim, then Suzy must have 27 pencils. This is our target. Circle it. 27 is the number that we want to get when we plug in 4 for q in our answer choices.

Step 3: Plug into answer choices.

We are looking for the answer choice that would be equal to 27 when we plug in 4 for q.

(A) $\dfrac{q}{23} = \dfrac{4}{23}$

(B) $q - 23 = 4 - 23 = -19$

(C) $q + 23 = 4 + 23 = 27$

(D) $23 - q = 23 - 4 = 19$

Choice C gives us 27, which is what we were looking for, so we choose C and answer the question correctly.

There are not too many of this problem type on the ISEE. However, if you read through a problem and think, "this would be a lot easier if they gave us real numbers", then make up your own numbers! Sometimes the process of solving with real numbers will be enough to figure out what the correct answer is.

- If you think to yourself, "this problem would be a lot easier with real numbers", then plug in real numbers

Strategy #3: If they ask for the value of a variable, plug in answer choices

On the ISEE, it is often easier to plug in answer choices and see what works. In particular, you may find this strategy most helpful on word problems. After all, this is a multiple-choice test so one of those answers has to work!

- Can often use this strategy on word problems
- This is a multiple-choice test

For this strategy, keep in mind that a variable is not always a letter. The problem might define x as the number of cars, or it might just ask you what the number of cars is. Either way, it is still asking for the value of a variable and you can use this strategy. The test writers might also throw in a symbol, such as a small square, instead of a letter.

- A variable may not always be a letter, it can be any unknown quantity
- Sometimes there is a symbol, such as a small square, instead of a letter

Here are a couple of examples:

1. In the equation $3 \times (\blacksquare + 5) = 18$, what number could replace $\blacksquare$?

   (A) 1
   (B) 2
   (C) 3
   (D) 4

2. A pet store divided their mice into cages. If each cage has the same number of mice in it and there are 6 cages, which could be the total number of mice that the pet store has?

   (A) 11
   (B) 15
   (C) 21
   (D) 24

Answers:

1. The question asks for the value of a variable, so we can plug in answer choices for that variable and see which one works. If we plug in answer choice A (1) for ■, then we get 3 × (1 + 5) = 18. If we simplify this, we get 3 × 6 = 18. The value of the left side of the equation is equal to the value of the right side of the equation so answer choice A is correct.

2. They are asking for the total number. Even though this is not a letter, it is still an unknown quantity and therefore we can plug in answer choices. Let's try out answer choice A. If there were 11 mice and we tried to divide them evenly into 6 cages, we would wind up with partial mice. Ew! From this, we can see that the number of mice must be divisible by 6 without a remainder. Only choice D (24) is evenly divisible by 6 so it is the correct answer.

Those are the basic strategies that you need to know for the math section. As you go through the content sections, you will learn content and the strategies that work for specific problem types.

Workouts

Now that you have the strategies, it is time to head to the workouts!

The format of each workout is very predictable so that you can focus on the material and not the directions.

Here is what you should look for:

Vocabulary

Each workout begins with a vocabulary section that has:

- Roots and words with those roots. Be sure to memorize the roots because there will be different words in later workouts with those same roots. After each word there is a space for you to write in an example sentence or memory trick – whatever will help you to remember the meaning of the word. There are also 1-2 questions to help you learn the roots.
- Words to remember. Each workout has three words that you need to memorize. There are also 1-2 questions about these words to help you make associations to remember these words.

Verbal Reasoning practice

The next section of each workout contains practice questions for the Verbal Reasoning section.

- Practice for both synonyms and sentence completions.
- You will be expected to also learn and apply strategy as you move through these practice questions.

Reading Comprehension practice

The next section of each workout gives you practice for the Reading Comprehension section.

- You will start out in workouts #1-#3 by identifying specific and general questions.
- Workouts #4-#15 have one reading passage each followed by questions for you to answer. These are just like the passages that will be on the test.

Math practice

The final section of each workout has practice for the Quantitative Reasoning and Mathematics Achievement sections:

- The focus of these sections is covering as much of the content as possible. Be sure to understand why you missed questions before moving on to the next workout.
- Each workout has one question from each of the following categories:

  - whole numbers and operations
  - fractions and decimals
  - algebra
  - geometry and measurement
  - data and probability

You may notice that you will be asked to write down strategies as well as correct answers. Please do NOT skip the strategy part. The goal of this book is to make success automatic, so you have to practice. Gradually the book will transition from telling you all of the strategies beforehand to having you complete a checklist after you are done. There is a method to this madness – the repetition will make the strategies stick even with the pressure of test day.

Also, make flashcards for words and roots that you do not know and practice them frequently! Take them everywhere with you.

Now go get 'em!

Vocabulary

Roots

Below are some roots. I will give you the definition of the root and then two examples of words that have that root. I will give you the definition of each word and then you need to write in an example sentence or a memory trick you will use to remember the meaning of the word. At the end of the roots section, I will ask a question or two that gets you thinking about the roots and their meanings. Then we have the "Words to Remember!" section. These are three words that you need to memorize – I will give you the words and an example sentence, and then you need to answer a question or two about the words.

Be sure to make flashcards (or keep a list) of any words that you don't know. You will be responsible for knowing and applying the definitions of all the roots and words that you have learned as you move through the workouts.

Root: *cis*
Definition – to cut
Examples:
Excise – to cut out
Sentence or memory trick:

Concise – brief and to the point (no extra words are used)
Sentence or memory trick:

Root: *con*
Definition – together or with
Examples:
Condense – to make more dense and shorter
Sentence or memory trick:

Consult – to seek advice from someone
Sentence or memory trick:

Roots questions

1. In the word *concise*, what is being cut out?

2. How does the word *condense* relate to meaning of the *con* root?

Words to remember!

Flourish – to grow successfully
Example: Stewart was able to take an expensive vacation since his business has flourished this year.

Quaint – old-fashioned and charming
Example: The quaint town in the mountains drew many visitors to its cobblestone streets and Victorian houses.

Bloated – swollen or inflated
Example: After eating three large plates of spaghetti, Camille felt very bloated.

Words to Remember Question:
Would you want poison ivy to flourish in your backyard? Why or why not?

Verbal Reasoning practice

Synonyms strategy review

If you know the word, think of a definition and jot it down before you look at the answer choices. If you have heard the word but can't define it:

- Use positive or negative – write a "+" or "–" sign next to the question word and then rule out answer choices that are opposite or neutral
- Use context – in what sentence or phrase have you heard the word before?
- Look for roots and word parts – ask yourself what other words this word looks like

Synonyms practice

Before you answer each question write beside it which strategy you will use.

1. INCISION: Strategy:

   (A) cut
   (B) instrument
   (C) proof
   (D) target

2. CONNECT: Strategy:

   (A) abandon
   (B) gain
   (C) join
   (D) succeed

3. QUAINT: Strategy:

   (A) astounding
   (B) disguised
   (C) premium
   (D) old-fashioned

4. BLOATED: Strategy:

   (A) irritated
   (B) marvelous
   (C) swollen
   (D) tough

Sentence Completions strategy review

Our basic strategies for sentence completions are:

- First underline the key idea – every sentence completion question has a key idea
- Look for sentences showing contrast and circle any conjunctions that are used to change direction ("however", "but", "although", "even though", "despite")
- Look for sentences showing cause or sequence – these sentences may have the word "because" or words indicating time such as "while" and "after"
- Use our strategies for synonyms when you don't know the meaning of one or more of the answer choices

Sentence Completions practice

1. Although plants frequently wilt when they are moved, with a little water and sunshine they bounce back and even --------.

   (A) decorate
   (B) flourish
   (C) proceed
   (D) wither

2. William Strunk, Jr., wrote a book that encouraged ------ writing, or writing that does not use any unnecessary words.

   (A) concise
   (B) graceful
   (C) personal
   (D) steady

3. The composer Joseph Haydn thought his understanding of music theory was lacking so he --------.

   (A) played many instruments
   (B) grew up in Austria
   (C) taught himself the fundamentals needed for composing music
   (D) played music for the king

Reading Comprehension practice

Reading strategy review

Before reading any passages:

- Plan your time – know your start time, end time, and when you should finish each passage
- Prioritize passages – don't just answer the passages in the order given

Before you read a passage:

- Go to the questions first and mark them "S" for specific or "G" for general and underline what the question asks about if it is a specific question (keep in mind that for some specific questions there is nothing to underline)

After you read the passage:

- Answer specific questions first
- Answer general questions last
- On specific questions look out for answer choices that twist words from the passage
- On general questions watch out for answer choices that are details and not the main idea

Reading passage practice

We are going to work on identifying questions as specific or general before we jump into full passages. Mark each question below with an "S" or "G". If it is a specific question, underline what the question asks about (keep in mind that not every specific question has something to underline).

1. The main purpose of this passage is to

2. The passage implies that lawn watering is

3. In line 8, the word "dawn" most nearly means

4. According to the author, how did irrigation change farming?

5. Which question could be answered with information in the passage?

Math practice

Quantitative Reasoning and Mathematics Achievement strategies

Our basic strategies for the math sections on the ISEE are:

- Estimate – this is a multiple-choice test!
- If there are variables in the answer choices, try plugging in your own numbers
- If they ask for the value of a variable, plug in answer choices

Quantitative Reasoning and Mathematics Achievement practice

1. Use the number set below to answer the question.

   $$\{4, 6, 8, 9, 10, \ldots\}$$

   Which term best describes the numbers in this set?

   (A) even numbers
   (B) odd numbers
   (C) composite numbers
   (D) prime numbers

2. Use the shapes below to answer the question.

   What fraction of the above shapes are circles?

   (A) $\dfrac{1}{12}$

   (B) $\dfrac{1}{6}$

   (C) $\dfrac{1}{4}$

   (D) $\dfrac{1}{3}$

3. A number machine accepts numbers as inputs, performs an identical operation on each number, and then produces an output number.

Input	Output
2	3
3	5
5	9
10	19
25	49

Which input would create an output of 59?

(A) 25
(B) 27
(C) 30
(D) 35

4. Use the pictures below to answer the question.

| J | Q | Q | K | A |

| K | A | A | J | K |

If a card is randomly chosen, what are the odds it will have a "Q" on it?

(A) 1 in 10
(B) 1 in 5
(C) 1 in 4
(D) 2 in 5

5. The perimeter of the rectangle below is 18 cm. The length is 4 cm, as shown.

What is the width of this rectangle?

(A) 5 cm
(B) 6 cm
(C) 8 cm
(D) 10 cm

Workout #1 Answers

Vocabulary

Roots questions

1. The extra words are being cut out. If a person is concise, they don't use any unnecessary words.

2. If something is condensed, it is squished together to make it smaller.

Words to remember question

1. No. If poison ivy flourished there would be a lot of it in your backyard which would mean you couldn't play there.

Verbal Reasoning practice

Synonyms practice

1. A is the correct answer. The word *incision* has the *cis* root in it which means "cut", so an *incision* is a cut.

2. C is the correct answer. The word *connect* has the *con* root in it which means "together" or "with". Since the word *join* means "to put things together", it is the correct answer choice.

3. D is the correct answer. This was one of the words to remember – if you missed this one make sure you study the vocabulary words before you do the verbal practice section.

4. C is the correct answer. This was also a word to remember – please review the words to remember if you missed this one.

Sentence Completions practice

1. B is the correct answer choice. This is a sentence that shows contrast. We would underline "frequently wilt" because that is what the first part of the sentence is about. Then we would circle the word "although" because that tells us we are looking for the opposite of *frequently wilt*. The word *wither* is a synonym for *wilt*, so we can rule out choice D. The word *decorate* isn't related to *wilt*, so we can rule out choice A as well. *Proceed* means "to go forward" which could kind of work, but the word *flourish* is a much better fit for having a meaning that is the opposite of *wilt* so answer choice B is the best answer.

2. A is the correct answer choice. For this question, we would underline "writing that does not use any unnecessary words" since this restates whatever word belongs in the blank. Since *concise* means "brief and to the point", it is the correct answer.

3. C is the correct answer choice. The word "so" tells us that this is a sentence showing cause. What would Haydn do if he lacked music theory? He would teach himself what he needed to know.

Reading Comprehension practice

Reading passage practice

1. G – This is a general question. The word *main* usually indicates a general question.

2. S – This is a specific question. It is asking about a specific detail and not the main idea. You should have underlined "lawn watering" since that is what you are looking for.

3. S – This is a specific question. Any time a question refers to a particular line, it is always a specific question. You should have underlined "line 8" and "dawn" since that is what you would look for in the passage.

4. S – This is a specific question. Although it may seem like this could be specific or general, on this test if a question begins with "according to the author" or "according to the passage", it is a specific question. We would underline "irrigation" since we are looking for where the passage talks about irrigation.

5. S – This is a specific question. This is one of those specific questions where there is nothing to underline. The details here are in the answer choices and not the question.

Math practice

Quantitative Reasoning and Mathematics Achievement practice

1. C is the correct answer choice. It is very tempting to choose answer choice A since most of the numbers are even. However, the number 9 is not even. Composite numbers are numbers that have factors other than themselves and 1 and each of the numbers in the set has factors other than themselves and 1.

2. D is the correct answer choice. There are a total of 12 shapes and 4 of them are circles. This means that $\frac{4}{12}$ of the shapes are circles. This fraction must be reduced however. If we divide both the numerator and denominator by 4 then we get $\frac{1}{3}$.

3. C is the correct answer choice. In order to answer this question, we need to figure out the operation that is performed on the input to get the output number. If we look at just the first set of numbers, we might think that the rule is to add 1. However, if we apply this rule to the second input, we get an output of 4, which is not the case. The same rule must apply to all the inputs and outputs. If we play around with different operations, we find that multiplying by 2 and then subtracting 1 is the operation that is performed on each input. The tricky part is that we have to work backwards to get the input when given the output. The easiest way to do this is simply to plug in answer choices as the input and see which one gives us an output of 59. If we apply the rule to answer choice A, we would get $(25 \times 2) - 1 = 50 - 1 = 49$. Since this is not 59, we can rule out answer choice A. If we try answer choice B, we would get $(27 \times 2) - 1 = 53$, so we can rule out choice B. Now let's try choice C. If we plug in 30 as our input, we would get $(30 \times 2) - 1 = 59$. Since this is the desired output, answer choice C is correct.

4. B is the correct answer choice. This is a basic probability question. In order to find the chance of a type of card being chosen, we figure out how many of those cards exist out of the total. Since there are 2 cards with "Q" on them out of a total 10 cards, the chance of drawing a "Q" is 2 out of 10. This is not an answer choice, however, because probabilities can be reduced just like a fraction can. We can divide both 2 and 10 by 2 and we get that the chance of drawing a "Q" is 1 in 5.

5. A is the correct answer choice. To find the perimeter of a rectangle we need to add two lengths and two widths. Since the length of the rectangle is 4 cm, adding two lengths gives us 8 cm. In order to get to a perimeter of 18 cm, the two widths would have to add up to 10 cm. That means that one width is 5 cm.

Workout #2

Vocabulary

Roots

Below are some roots. I will give you the definition of the root and then two examples of words that have that root. I will give you the definition of each word and then you need to write in an example sentence or a memory trick you will use to remember the meaning of the word. At the end of the roots section, I will ask a question or two that gets you thinking about the roots and their meanings. Then we have the "Words to Remember!" section. These are three words that you need to memorize – I will give you the words and an example sentence, and then you need to answer a question or two about the words.

Be sure to make flashcards (or keep a list) of any words that you don't know. You will be responsible for knowing and applying the definitions of all the roots and words that you have learned as you move through the workouts.

Root: *hes*
Definition – to stick
Examples:
Adhesive – sticky
Sentence or memory trick:

Cohesive – sticking together well
Sentence or memory trick:

Root: *lib*
Definition – free
Examples:
Liberate – to free
Sentence or memory trick:

Liberty – freedom
Sentence or memory trick:

Roots questions

1. What is adhesive tape?

2. What do you think the root *co* means in the word *cohesive*? (hint: it is related to the *con* root that we had in the last lesson)

Words to remember!

Frigid – really, really cold
Example: You should really bundle up on a frigid morning so that you do not get frostbite.

Drench – to soak
Example: An unexpected rain shower left me drenched since I had no umbrella.

Ponder – to reflect upon or think about something deeply
Example: Lindsay often pondered what she wanted to be when she grew up.

Words to Remember Question:
What would happen if you got drenched on a frigid day?

Verbal Reasoning practice

Synonyms strategy review

Our basic strategies for synonyms are: (fill in the blanks below)

If you know the word, think of a definition and jot it down before you look at the answer choices.
If you have heard the word but can't define it:

- Use positive or negative – write a (1)_____next to the question word and then rule out answer choices that are opposite or neutral
- Use context – (2)_____?
- Look for (3)_____ – ask yourself what other words this word looks like

Synonyms practice

Before you answer each question write beside it which strategy you will use.

1. LIBERATING: Strategy:

   (A) bloated
   (B) freeing
   (C) peculiar
   (D) relaxed

2. ADHESIVE: Strategy:

   (A) drenched
   (B) flourishing
   (C) quaint
   (D) sticky

3. FRIGID: Strategy:

   (A) freezing
   (B) public
   (C) soaked
   (D) waddling

4. CONGREGATE: Strategy:

   (A) demonstrate
   (B) excise
   (C) gather
   (D) undertake

Sentence Completions strategy review

Our basic strategies for sentence completions are: (fill in the blanks below)

- First underline (1)_____ – every sentence completion question has a key idea
- Look for sentences showing (2)_____ and circle any conjunctions that are used to change direction ("however", "but", "although", "even though", "despite")

- Look for sentences showing (3)_____ – these sentences may have the word "because" or words indicating time such as "while" and "after"
- Use our (4)_____ when you don't know the meaning of one or more of the answer choices

Sentence Completions practice

1. After a major fish kill, dead and ------- fish can wash up on shore for many days.

   (A) bloated
   (B) cohesive
   (C) incisive
   (D) twirling

2. The crying toddler was -------- and instantly calmed down when his mother put him in her lap.

   (A) absurd
   (B) consoled
   (C) frigid
   (D) vague

3. Although bluegrass music is known for being a uniquely American creation, it --------.

   (A) was first created in the mountains of the eastern United States
   (B) featured violins, or fiddles, played in a new way
   (C) introduced a new vocal style as well
   (D) was heavily influenced by the music of Ireland and Scotland

Reading Comprehension practice

Reading strategy review

Before reading any passages: (fill in the blanks below)

- Plan your time – know your (1)_____, and when you should finish each passage
- Prioritize passages – don't just answer the passages (2)_____

Before you read a passage:

- Go to the questions first and mark them (3)_____and underline what the question asks about if it is a (4)_____(keep in mind that for some specific questions there is nothing to underline)

After you read the passage:

- Answer (5)_____questions first
- Answer (6)_____questions last
- On specific questions look out for answer choices that (7)_____
- On general questions watch out for answer choices that are (8)_____

Reading passage practice

We are going to work on identifying questions as specific or general before we jump into full passages. Mark each question below with an "S" or "G". If it is a specific question, underline what the question asks about (keep in mind that not every specific question has something to underline).

1. Which best summarizes the main idea of the passage?

2. Which term best characterizes the tree growth in the Amazon that is described in the passage?

3. It can be inferred from the passage that mass extinction would be

4. In the third paragraph (lines 15-19), the author implies that the destruction of the tree canopy would

5. The purpose of the second paragraph (lines 7-13) is

Math practice

Quantitative Reasoning and Mathematics Achievement strategies

Our basic strategies for the math sections on the ISEE are: (fill in the blanks below)

- (1)_____ – this is a multiple-choice test!
- If there are variables in the answer choices, try (2)_____.
- If they ask for the value of a variable, (3)_____.

Quantitative Reasoning and Mathematics Achievement practice

1. Dianne wants to order cupcakes for a party so that every guest will get one cupcake. She knows how many guests are coming and how many cupcakes are in a box. Which equation will help her figure out how many boxes (b) of cupcakes she needs to buy?

    (A) b = number of boxes × number of cupcakes in a box
    (B) b = number of boxes ÷ number of cupcakes in a box
    (C) b = number of guests + number of cupcakes in a box
    (D) b = number of guests ÷ number of cupcakes in a box

2. Lucas combined the following ingredients.

    4 cups orange juice
    2 cups cranberry juice
    3 cups grapefruit juice
    1 cup lemon juice
    6 cups apple juice

    He then divided this juice mixture evenly among six glasses. About how many cups of juice were in each glass?

    (A) 2

    (B) $2\frac{1}{2}$

    (C) 3

    (D) $3\frac{1}{2}$

3. Renee has a box with 80 cookies in it. The cookies are grouped into packages. If each package has 10 cookies in it, which equation would help Renee figure out how many packages (p) she has?

(A) $p = 80 \div 10$
(B) $p + 10 = 80$
(C) $80 - p = 10$
(D) $p \div 10 = 80$

4. Ms. Glover's class is going to collect data from a bake sale and then make bar graphs showing the results. Below are some of the ideas they had for data that would be appropriate to display in a bar graph.

Data From Bake Sale
1. Number of brownies sold each hour
2. Cookie sales by different types of cookies
3. ?

Which type of data could be added to this list?

(A) names of students who bought cookies
(B) kinds of muffins sold
(C) dollar amount of sales for each hour
(D) colors of items sold

5. Which pair of shapes below have the same number of lines of symmetry?

(A)

(B)

(C)

(D)

Workout #2 Answers

Vocabulary

Roots questions

1. Tape that sticks to something, such as packing tape, Scotch tape, etc.

2. The root *co* means "together".

Words to remember question

1. You would probably get sick if you were soaking wet on a really, really cold day.

Verbal Reasoning practice

Synonyms strategy review

1. "+" or "–" sign

2. in what sentence or phrase have you heard the word before

3. roots or word parts

Synonyms practice

1. B is the correct answer choice. The word *liberating* has the root *lib* which means "free".

2. D is the correct answer choice. The word *adhesive* has the root *hes* which means "to stick". You could also use context – *adhesive tape* is a name for tape that sticks to things.

3. A is the correct answer choice. This was in the words to learn section from this workout – please review those words if you missed this question.

4. C is the correct answer choice. The word *congregate* has the *con* root which means "together" or "with". Since *gather* means "to come together" that is the answer choice that most closely relates to the meaning of the root.

Sentence Completions strategy review

1. the key idea

2. contrast

3. cause or sequence

4. strategies for synonyms

Sentence Completions practice

1. A is the correct answer choice. This is a sentence that shows cause or sequence. What would fish look like after a fish kill? It wouldn't make sense to say that they were *cohesive* (sticking together as a group) or *incisive* (cutting), so we can eliminate choices B and C. A dead fish could be *twirling*, but if you think of the result of a fish kill, *twirling* is not what would come to mind so answer choice D is out. A dead fish would be *swollen* or *bloated*, however, so choice A is correct.

2. B is the correct answer choice. This is another sentence showing cause or sequence. What would be the result of a crying child sitting in his mother's lap? It would not make sense that the child would be made *absurd, frigid,* or *vague* by this action, so we can eliminate choices A, C, and D. To *console* another person is to make him or her feel better, so answer choice B would be the most direct result.

3. D is the correct answer choice. The first step is to circle the word "although" – this is a conjunction letting us know that the second half of the sentence will be different from the first half. Now we have to underline the key idea in the first half of the sentence. The first half of the sentence talks about bluegrass being "uniquely American". We are looking for an answer choice that contradicts being "uniquely American". Answer choices B and C don't relate to whether or not the music form is American. Answer choice A goes along with bluegrass being American so we can eliminate it. Answer choice D contradicts bluegrass being uniquely American.

Reading Comprehension practice
Reading strategy review

1. start time, end time

2. in the order given

3. "S" for specific or "G" for general

4. specific question

5. specific

6. general

7. twist words from the passage

8. details and not the main idea

Reading practice

1. G – This question is general. The words "main idea" let us know it is a question about the passage as a whole.

2. S – This is a specific question. It asks about a detail from the passage. We would underline "tree growth in the Amazon" as what we are looking for in the passage.

3. S – This is a specific question. On this test, questions that use "infer" (or "imply") are looking for details. We would underline "mass extinction".

4. S – This is a specific question. Questions that have line references are always specific. We would underline "destruction of the tree canopy" and "lines 15-19".

5. S – This is a specific question. Questions with line references are specific. In this case, we underline the line numbers since those tell us where to find the answer to the question.

Math practice

Quantitative Reasoning and Mathematics Achievement strategies

1. Estimate

2. plugging in your own numbers

3. plug in answer choices

Quantitative Reasoning and Mathematics Achievement practice

1. D is the correct answer. In this question, we know the total (number of guests), the size of each group (number of cupcakes in a box), and we are looking for the number of groups (how many boxes are needed). In this situation we use division, so choices A and C are out. In choice B, we would have to divide the number of boxes by the number of cupcakes, but we are not given the number of boxes, so we cannot do that! We are left with answer choice D.

2. B is the correct answer choice. If we add all of the different juices together, we get a total of 16 cups of liquid. Now we have to divide this among 6 cups. This requires us to create a mixed number:

$$\frac{16}{6} = \frac{6}{6} + \frac{6}{6} + \frac{4}{6} = 2\frac{4}{6}$$

    The question asks "about how many cups" and $2\frac{4}{6}$ is closest to $2\frac{1}{2}$.

3. A is the correct answer choice. In this question, we are given the total, the size of each group, and then asked for the number of groups. This means that we use division, so we can eliminate choices B and C. In order to find how many groups we have, we should divide the total number of items by the size of each group. Answer choice D shows the number of groups divided by the size of each group, so we can eliminate choice D. Answer choice A correctly shows the total number of items being divided by the size of each group in order to determine the total number of groups.

4. C is the correct answer choice. The question tells us that the data needs to be represented in a bar chart. This means that we are looking for quantitative data (you get a number for answer) and not qualitative data (you are just listing categories). Only choice C gives you data that would be appropriate to create a bar graph from.

5. B is the correct answer choice. The best way to answer this question is to use ruling out. In choice A, a circle has many, many lines of symmetry but a square only has four so we can eliminate choice A. In choice B, we could divide both figures with a horizontal and a vertical line of symmetry only. Each figure has two lines of symmetry so B is the correct answer choice.

Workout #3

Vocabulary

Roots

Below are some roots. I will give you the definition of the root and then two examples of words that have that root. I will give you the definition of each word and then you need to write in an example sentence or a memory trick you will use to remember the meaning of the word. At the end of the roots section, I will ask a question or two that gets you thinking about the roots and their meanings. Then we have the "Words to Remember!" section. These are three words that you need to memorize – I will give you the words and an example sentence, and then you need to answer a question or two about the words.

Be sure to make flashcards (or keep a list) of any words that you don't know. You will be responsible for knowing and applying the definitions of all the roots and words that you have learned as you move through the workouts.

Root: *port*
Definition – to carry
Examples:
Transport – to move across a distance
Sentence or memory trick:

Import – to bring into a country
Sentence or memory trick:

Root: *sci*
Definition – to know
Examples:
Conscious – aware or aware of
Sentence or memory trick:

Omniscient – all-knowing
Sentence or memory trick:

Roots questions

1. If the word *transport* means "to move across a distance", what do you think the root *trans* means?

2. If the word *omniscient* means "all-knowing", what do you think the root *omni* means?

Words to remember!

Barren – describes a place where nothing is growing
Example: The abandoned parking lot was a barren wasteland of concrete.

Urgent – needing immediate action or response
Example: The urgent care clinic sees patients with medical problems that need to be taken care of right away.

Emphasize – to make it clear that something is important
Example: Before I got on the school bus, my mother emphasized that I needed to hand in my homework in order to raise my grade.

Words to remember questions

1. Would you describe a jungle as being barren? Why or why not?

2. When is it urgent to put up your car window?

Verbal Reasoning practice

Synonyms strategy review

Our basic strategies for synonyms are: (fill in the blanks below)

If you know the word, think of a definition and jot it down before you look at the answer choices. If you have heard the word but can't define it:

- Use (1)_____ – write a "+" or "–" sign next to the question word and then rule out answer choices that are opposite or neutral
- Use context – in what sentence or phrase have you (2)_____?
- Look for roots and word parts – ask yourself (3)_____

Synonyms practice

Before you answer each question write beside it which strategy you will use.

1. TRANSPORT: Strategy:

   (A) confide
   (B) drench
   (C) move
   (D) stagger

2. DRENCH: Strategy:

   (A) consult
   (B) examine
   (C) liberate
   (D) soak

3. UNCONSCIOUS: Strategy:

   (A) barren
   (B) concise
   (C) thriving
   (D) unknowing

4. PRESCIENCE: Strategy:

   (A) foreknowledge
   (B) material
   (C) reminder
   (D) service

Sentence Completions strategy review

Our basic strategies for sentence completions are: (fill in the blanks below)

- First underline the key idea – (1)_____question has a key idea
- Look for sentences showing contrast and circle any conjunctions that are (2)_____ ("however", "but", "although", "even though", "despite")
- Look for sentences showing cause or sequence – these sentences may have the word (3)_____or words indicating time such as (4)_____
- Use our strategies for synonyms when (5)_____ one or more of the answer choices

Sentence Completions practice

1. Harold owned a(n) -------- business that shipped paper products to countries such as China, India, and Japan.

   (A) barren
   (B) export
   (C) quaint
   (D) reasonable

2. When solving a complex problem, it is important to spend time ------- different solutions.

   (A) ditching
   (B) irrigating
   (C) pondering
   (D) urging

3. Although the artist Woody Jackson is best known for his paintings of cows, he also ---------.

    (A)   produced many landscape paintings of farmland
    (B)   lives in Vermont
    (C)   attended art school
    (D)   has five sons

Reading Comprehension practice

Reading strategy review

Answer the questions below:

1. What should you do before you start your first passage?

2. Once you decide to work on a passage, what should you do before reading?

3. Which questions should you answer first – specific or general?

4. What kind of answers do you need to look out for on specific questions?

5. What kind of answers do you need to look out for on general questions?

Reading passage practice

We are going to work on identifying questions as specific or general before we jump into full passages. Mark each question below with an "S" or "G". If it is a specific question, underline what the question asks about (keep in mind that not every specific question has something to underline).

1. The primary purpose of this passage is to

2. In line 14, the word "confounded" comes closest in meaning to

3. Which of the following can be inferred from the first sentence (lines 1-2)?

4. According to the passage, chariots were first used by

5. Which question can be answered with information in the passage?

Math practice

Quantitative Reasoning and Mathematics Achievement strategies

Our basic strategies for the math sections on the ISEE are: (fill in the blanks below)

- Estimate – (1)_____!
- If there are (2)_____, try plugging in your own numbers
- If they ask for (3)_____, plug in answer choices

Quantitative Reasoning and Mathematics Achievement practice

1. Which answer choice gives the standard form for the number five hundred thirty thousand one hundred six?

   (A) 530,106
   (B) 530,160
   (C) 531,106
   (D) 531,006

2. Which number is equivalent to $\dfrac{9}{100}$?

   (A) 0.0009
   (B) 0.009
   (C) 0.09
   (D) 0.9

3. Use the given equations.

   $$A + 6 = 9$$
   $$B + 3 = 9$$

   What is the value of $B - A$?

   (A) 2
   (B) 3
   (C) 6
   (D) 9

4. Sylvia has a bouquet of flowers that contains only white, red, purple, and yellow flowers. There are 7 white flowers, 3 red flowers, 8 purple flowers, and 6 yellow flowers. If a flower were randomly selected, which color flower has a 1 in 3 chance of being selected?

(A) white
(B) red
(C) purple
(D) yellow

5. Alexander had a square piece of paper that was 6 inches on each side. He cut a square out of the center that was 2 inches on each side, shown as the darker shaded region in Figure 1.

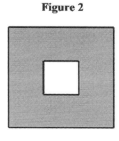

What was the area of the remaining piece of paper, as shown in Figure 2?

(A) 4 in²
(B) 8 in²
(C) 16 in²
(D) 32 in²

Workout #3 Answers

Vocabulary

Roots questions

1. The root *trans* means "across".

2. The root *omni* means "all". For example, an omnivore eats all kinds of food.

Words to remember questions

1. No. Many different types of plants and animals live in the jungle so it is the opposite of barren.

2. Any time there is bad weather, such as rain or strong winds, you should put up your car window immediately.

Verbal Reasoning practice

Synonyms strategy review

1. positive or negative

2. heard the word before

3. what other words this word looks like

Synonyms practice

1. C is the correct answer choice. The word *transport* has the root *port* which means "to carry". The word *move* comes closest to the meaning of this root.

2. D is the correct answer choice. This is a word to remember from workout #2 – please review those words if you missed this question.

3. D is the correct answer choice. The word *conscious* has two roots – *con* which means "with" and *sci* which means "to know" – so *conscious* means "with knowing". The root *un* tells us that we want the opposite of "with knowing", so *unknowing* works.

4. A is the correct answer choice. The word *prescience* has two roots – *pre* which means "before" and *sci* which means "to know" – and *foreknowledge* combines these two meanings. You may not have known the word *foreknowledge*, but sometimes we have to choose words that have parts that we recognize even if we don't know the whole word.

Sentence Completions strategies

1. every sentence completion

2. used to change direction

3. because

4. while and after

5. you don't know the meaning of

Sentence Completions practice

1. B is the correct answer choice. The question sentence tells us that the business shipped products to other countries and *export* literally means "to carry out" – *ex* means "out" and *port* means "to carry".

2. C is the correct answer choice. To *ponder* means to "think about", so it is exactly what you would want to do when solving a complex problem. This is a word to remember from workout #2, so please review those words if you missed this question.

3. A is the correct answer choice. In this sentence, the beginning talks about paintings of cows. The word *although* tells us that there will be some contrast. However, the end of the sentence still needs to relate to paintings in order to match the beginning of the sentence.

Reading Comprehension practice

Reading strategy review

1. Plan out the time for each passage and decide in what order to answer passages.

2. Go to the questions and mark them "G" for general or "S" for specific (you should also underline key words if a specific question has them).

3. Specific.

4. Answers that twist words from the passage so that the meaning is different.

5. Answers that provide details from the passage but are not the main idea.

Reading passage practice

1. G – This is a general question. The words "primary purpose" let us know that it is about the passage as a whole.

2. S – This is a specific question. We would underline the line number and "confounded" since that is what we are looking for.

3. S – This is a specific question. Any question with a line reference is a specific question and we would underline the line numbers since that is where we will look for the answer.

4. S – This is a specific question. It is asking for a detail about chariots, so we would underline "chariots were first used".

5. S – This is a specific question. In this case, we are looking for the details in the answer choices, and not in the question, so there is nothing to underline in the question.

Math practice

Quantitative Reasoning and Mathematics Achievement strategies

1. this is a multiple-choice test

2. variables in the answer choices

3. the value of a variable

Quantitative Reasoning and Mathematics Achievement practice

1. A is the correct answer choice. We have to remember that if a place value is not mentioned in the written form, then we must mark it with a 0 in the standard form. Only answer choice A puts each number in the correct place value position.

2. C is the correct answer choice. The fraction $\frac{9}{100}$ tells us that there should be a 9 in the hundredths place. We just need to remember to mark the other places with a zero.

3. B is the correct answer choice. In order to answer this question we first have to solve for A and B. Here is what the math looks like:

$$A + 6 = 9$$
$$\underline{-6 \quad -6}$$
$$A = 3$$
$$B + 3 = 9$$
$$\underline{-3 \quad -3}$$
$$B = 6$$

Now we substitute these values of A and B into the expression:

$$B - A = 6 - 3 = 3$$

4. C is the correct answer choice. Our first step in answering this question is to add up the total number of flowers. There are a total of 24 flowers. Now we can set up a proportion to figure out which flower color has a 1 in 3 chance of being selected.

$$\frac{1}{3} = \frac{f \text{ flowers}}{24 \text{ total flowers}}$$

Now we cross-multiply to solve:

$$1 \times 24 = 3 \times f$$
$$24 = 3f$$
$$8 = f$$

We now know that we are looking for the flower color that has 8 flowers in the bouquet. There are 8 purple flowers so choice C is correct.

5. D is the correct answer choice. This is a "shaded regions" problem. In order to answer these questions, we find the area of a larger figure and then subtract the area that is not included to find the other area. In this case, the area of the larger square is:

$$6 \text{ in} \times 6 \text{ in} = 36 \text{ in}^2$$

The area of the shaded region that was removed is:

$$2 \text{ in} \times 2 \text{ in} = 4 \text{ in}^2$$

Now we subtract the area of the shaded region from the area of the original square piece of paper and get:

$$36 \text{ in}^2 - 4\text{in}^2 = 32\text{in}^2$$

Vocabulary

Roots

Below are some roots. I will give you the definition of the root and then two examples of words that have that root. I will give you the definition of each word and then you need to write in an example sentence or a memory trick you will use to remember the meaning of the word. At the end of the roots section, I will ask a question or two that gets you thinking about the roots and their meanings. Then we have the "Words to Remember!" section. These are three words that you need to memorize – I will give you the words and an example sentence, and then you need to answer a question or two about the words.

Be sure to make flashcards (or keep a list) of any words that you don't know. You will be responsible for knowing and applying the definitions of all the roots and words that you have learned as you move through the workouts.

Root: *cline*
Definition – to lean
Examples:
Incline – to lean towards (it can mean physically or when making a decision)
Sentence or memory trick:

Recline – to lean back
Sentence or memory trick:

Root: *luc/lum*
Definition: – light
Examples:
Luminous – glowing
Sentence or memory trick:

Translucent – letting light through
Sentence or memory trick:

Roots question

1. Do you remember what the root *trans* means? How does this relate to the word *translucent*?

Words to remember!

Folly – foolishness or a foolish action
Example: It was a folly to put all of my money into a business that made socks for worms.

Elated – very happy
Example: Earl was elated when he was accepted at his number one choice for independent school.

Humane – kind and full of sympathy for other living creatures
Example: Zachary volunteered at the Humane Society caring for dogs that did not have a home or family to care for them.

Words to remember questions

1. Would you feel elated or humane if you got to go on a really nice vacation?

2. Sometimes students put on performances called "follies". What do you think describes the acts are that performed at the "follies"?

Verbal Reasoning practice

Synonyms strategy review

Our basic strategies for synonyms are:

If you know the word, think of a definition and jot it down before you look at the answer choices. If you have heard the word but can't define it:

- Use positive or negative – write a "+" or "–" sign next to the question word and then rule out answer choices that are opposite or neutral
- Use context – in what sentence or phrase have you heard the word before?
- Look for roots and word parts – ask yourself what other words this word looks like

Synonyms practice

Before you answer each question write beside it which strategy you will use.

1. DECLINE: Strategy:

    (A) downturn
    (B) incision
    (C) permit
    (D) taunt

2. URGENT: Strategy:

    (A) cohesive
    (B) flourishing
    (C) important
    (D) luminous

3. LIBERTY: Strategy:

    (A) conscience
    (B) freedom
    (C) objective
    (D) transportation

4. LUMINOUS: Strategy:

    (A) condensed
    (B) liberal
    (C) portable
    (D) shining

Sentence Completions strategy review

Our basic strategies for sentence completions are:

*   First underline the key idea – every sentence completion question has a key idea
*   Look for sentences showing contrast and circle any conjunctions that are used to change direction ("however", "but", "although", "even though", "despite")

- Look for sentences showing cause or sequence – these sentences may have the word "because" or words indicating time such as "while" and "after"
- Use our strategies for synonyms when you don't know the meaning of one or more of the answer choices

Sentence Completions practice

1. In order to succeed on the battlefield as a unit, a battalion must have ------ among its members.

    (A) cohesion
    (B) folly
    (C) incline
    (D) suspicion

2. After a drought, many countries have to -------- food until they can build up their own crops again.

    (A) confess
    (B) decline
    (C) import
    (D) petrify

3. Although the contest was supposed to be very popular, in the end ---------.

    (A) a fifth grader won
    (B) there were very few entries
    (C) many students entered
    (D) the last entry came just before the deadline

Reading Comprehension practice

Reading passage practice

Now we will move onto answering questions about passages. As you work through the passage on the next page, please remember to:

- Mark questions "S" or "G" before you read the passage
- Answer specific questions first and then general questions
- Use ruling out

Questions #1-5

1   The early stages of modern human flight began in June of 1783. That is when a
2 crowd watched breathlessly as an unmanned hot air balloon lifted into the air and flew
3 for over a mile. Mere months later, a second balloon, this one filled with animals, was
4 successfully launched. Hot air balloon flights grew more common and people joined in
5 the fun. Even today, people can ride in a hot air balloon for enjoyment.

6   As fun as a balloon ride was, it was evident that hot air ballooning was never going
7 to be a real form of air travel. In 1804, the next stage of flight graced the scene with the
8 invention of the glider. A glider is similar to an airplane in that it has wings, but a glider
9 has no engine. Gliders work by floating on the wind and using wind force to stay in the
10 air. People could, as with balloons, use gliders for short, enjoyable rides, but not for any
11 real travel.

12   Flight as we know it today all began with two brothers and a brilliant idea. The
13 Wright Brothers had followed the news of the glider with interest. They were confident
14 that if people could steer a glider and an engine was attached to something with wings,
15 that device truly could fly through the air. After gathering all the reading material they
16 could find about gliders, Orville and Wilbur Wright started building their own version
17 in Kitty Hawk, North Carolina.

18   Their plan to build a glider that people could steer was successful to an extent.
19 After three years of work, they were able to create a glider that a man could steer while
20 flying. However, steering it in the wind was not easy at all. The brothers then took their
21 plan to the next stage and added an engine. Finally, in 1903, their new glider was ready
22 for a test flight.

23   Wilbur boarded this early airplane and flew for a few seconds before the glider
24 came to the ground. They took another test flight a few days later and were able to raise
25 the glider 120 feet into the air. Inspired, these brothers kept working for another 5 years.
26 In 1908, their invention developed to the point where it could fly for an hour.

27   Today, we can take flights across oceans and through time zones, all because of
28 these early stages of flight.

1. The main purpose of this passage is to

   (A) describe the invention of the hot air balloon.
   (B) discuss the invention of the glider.
   (C) relate the events that led up to modern air travel.
   (D) explain why Kitty Hawk was important to the Wright brothers.

2. The passages implies that early gliders

   (A) were first invented by the Romans.
   (B) could not be steered.
   (C) carried animals.
   (D) were all built by the Wright Brothers.

3. In line 23, the word "boarded" is closest in meaning to

   (A) climbed into.
   (B) covered up.
   (C) wooden.
   (D) forgotten.

4. According to the author, in June of 1783

   (A) a hot air balloon flew for over a mile.
   (B) a balloon filled with animals took flight.
   (C) humans first rode in hot air balloons.
   (D) the glider was invented.

5. Which question can be answered with information from the passage?

   (A) Where were the Wright brothers born?
   (B) In what country did the first hot air balloon fly?
   (C) Who was the first person to ride in a hot air balloon?
   (D) Did the original gliders have engines?

Math practice

Quantitative Reasoning and Mathematics Achievement strategies

Answer the questions below about strategy on the math sections:

1. What should we do because this is a multiple-choice test?

2. If there are variables in the answer choices, what should we do?

3. If they ask for the value of a variable, what should we do?

Quantitative Reasoning and Mathematics Achievement practice

1. What is the value of $4 \times (3 + 9) - 8$?

   (A) 13
   (B) 32
   (C) 38
   (D) 40

2. Cody bought one pretzel that cost $1.50, one soda that cost $1.75, one hamburger that cost $3.25, and one bag of potato chips. If he spent a total of $7.75, then how much did the potato chips cost?

   (A) $1.25
   (B) $1.50
   (C) $1.75
   (D) $2.25

3. Dolores is enlarging a photograph that is 4 inches wide by 6 inches long. If the width of the enlarged photograph is 14 inches, then what will the length be?

   (A) 15 inches
   (B) 16 inches
   (C) 18 inches
   (D) 21 inches

4. Mr. Arnold put blue and white chips in a bag. The chance that he would randomly pick a blue chip is 3 out 5. There are 12 white chips in the bag. How many blue chips are in the bag?

(A) 6
(B) 12
(C) 18
(D) 30

5. Hector wants to measure how much liquid a large plastic jug can hold. Which would be the most appropriate units for him to use?

(A) inches^2
(B) liters
(C) tablespoons
(D) kilometers

Workout #4 Answers

Vocabulary

Roots question

1. The root *trans* means "across", so the word *translucent* literally means "to let light across".

Words to remember questions:

1. You would probably be *elated* if you got to take a really nice vacation.

2. Acts performed at *follies* are foolish or silly.

Verbal Reasoning practice

Synonyms practice

1. A is the correct answer choice. The root *de* means "down" or "away" and *cline* means "to lean". Only *downturn* remotely relates to the meanings of these roots.

2. C is the correct answer choice. This is a word to remember from workout #3 so please review those words if you missed this question.

3. B is the correct answer choice. The word *liberty* has the root *lib* which means "free". You may have also been able to use context – what does the Statue of Liberty stand for?

4. D is the correct answer choice. The word *luminous* has the root *lum* which means "light".

Sentence Completions practice

1. A is the correct answer. For this question, it is helpful to use ruling out. Answer choices B and D can be ruled out because *folly* and *suspicion* would lead to the opposite of success on the battlefield. We can rule out answer choice C because *incline* (a slope) doesn't even make sense in this context. We are left with *cohesion*, which can refer to a group of people sticking together.

2. C is the correct answer. This is a cause or sequence relationship. If a country had a drought, that would cause them to do what with food? Get it from somewhere else – or import it.

3. B is the correct answer choice. This is a sentence showing contrast. The beginning of the sentence talks about how popular the contest was so we are looking for an answer choice that indicates the opposite, which answer choice B does.

Reading Comprehension practice

Reading Passage practice

1. C is the correct answer choice. This is a general question and the best place to find an answer for a general question is in the last sentence of the passage. The last sentence talks about how the early developments of hot air balloons and gliders led to modern air travel. Answer choice C repeats this idea.

2. B is the correct answer choice. The passage tells us that the Wright brothers were "confident that if people could steer a glider". The word "if" tells us that gliders before the Wright brothers could not be steered.

3. A is the correct answer choice. This is a vocabulary in context question and the best strategy here is to cross out the word "boarded" in the passage and then plug in answer choices and see which answer choice would not change the meaning of the sentence. If we do this, we can see that it only makes sense if Wilbur climbed into the plane.

4. A is the correct answer choice. If we go back to the passage, we can see that June of 1783 is when a hot air balloon flew over a mile. The other answer choices are very tempting because they were mentioned in the passage, but those events are not specifically mentioned as happening in June of 1783.

5. D is the correct answer. Since this is a specific question, we should be able to underline the correct answer in the passage. The passages tells us that "a glider has no engine", so answer choice D is correct.

Math practice

Quantitative Reasoning and Mathematics Achievement strategies

1. See if we can estimate before doing long calculations.

2. If there are variables in the answer choices, we should plug in our own numbers.

3. If they ask for the value of a variable, we should plug in answer choices and see what works.

Quantitative Reasoning and Mathematics Achievement practice

1. D is the correct answer choice. To answer this question we have to remember to follow the order of operations, also known as PEMDAS. We do what is in parentheses first, so:

$$4 \times (3 + 9) - 8 = 4 \times 12 - 8$$

Now we have to remember to do multiplication before subtraction:

$$4 \times 12 - 8 = 48 - 8 = 40$$

2. A is the correct answer choice. If we add together the prices that are known, we get a total of $6.50. If the total amount that he spent was $7.75 then we can subtract $6.50 from $7.75 to determine the price of the potato chips. Since $7.75 - $6.50 = $1.25, we know that the potato chips cost $1.25.

3. D is the correct answer choice. The best way to answer this question is to set up a proportion. One key for setting up a proportion is to label the top and bottom so that we can be sure that we are putting all the numbers in the correct place:

$$\frac{4 \text{ inches wide}}{6 \text{ inches long}} = \frac{14 \text{ inches wide}}{y \text{ inches long}}$$

Now we can use cross-multiplying to solve:

$$4 \times y = 6 \times 14$$
$$4y = 84$$
$$y = 21$$

The length must be 21 inches, or answer choice D.

4. C is the correct answer choice. This is a more involved problem type. We are given the probability of choosing one item type and the actual number of items for a different type of item. Our first step is to figure out the probability of choosing the item type that we have the actual number for. Since the chance of choosing a blue chip is 3 out of 5, the chance of choosing a white chip has to be 2 out of 5. Now that we have the probability of choosing a white chip, we can set up a proportion:

$$\frac{2 \text{ white chips}}{5 \text{ total chips}} = \frac{12 \text{ white chips}}{c \text{ total chips}}$$

Now we can cross-multiply to solve for the total number of chips:

$2 \times c = 5 \times 12$
$2c = 60$
$c = 30$

We aren't quite done yet – the question asked for the number of blue chips in the bag. We can subtract the number of white chips (12) from the total number of chips (30) and get that there are 18 blue chips.

5. B is the correct answer choice. First of all, we are measuring volume, so we can rule out choices A and D because they are not units of volume. Now we have to decide if it would be more appropriate to measure the liquid in a large jug with liters or tablespoons. If you tried to measure the contents of a large jug with tablespoons, you would be there a very long time trying to count all of those tablespoons. A liter is more appropriate.

Vocabulary

Roots

Below are some roots. I will give you the definition of the root and then two examples of words that have that root. I will give you the definition of each word and then you need to write in an example sentence or a memory trick you will use to remember the meaning of the word. At the end of the roots section, I will ask a question or two that gets you thinking about the roots and their meanings. Then we have the "Words to Remember!" section. These are three words that you need to memorize – I will give you the words and an example sentence, and then you need to answer a question or two about the words.

Be sure to make flashcards (or keep a list) of any words that you don't know. You will be responsible for knowing and applying the definitions of all the roots and words that you have learned as you move through the workouts.

Root: *flect/flex*
Definition – to bend
Examples:
Flexible – able to be bent
Sentence or memory trick:

Reflect – to turn or cast back (such as in a mirror)
Sentence or memory trick:

Root: *ver*
Definition – truth
Examples:
Verify – to provide evidence that something is true
Sentence or memory trick:

Verdict – a judgment or decision
Sentence or memory trick:

Roots questions

1. If the *de* root can mean "away", what does the word *deflect* mean?

2. How does the word *verdict* relate to the *ver* root?

Words to remember!

Essential – absolutely necessary
Example: It is essential that you drink enough water on a hot day in order to survive.

Lure – to attract or tempt
Example: Unfortunately, Bonnie was lured in by the promise of money that never appeared.

Sympathy – understanding or compassion
Example: Ginger felt sympathy for the poor hungry kitten.

Words to remember questions

1. When there is a snow day some employees are considered "essential personnel". What do you think this term means?

2. What is a fishing lure?

Verbal Reasoning practice

Synonyms strategy review

Our basic strategies for synonyms are:

If you know the word, think of a definition and jot it down before you look at the answer choices. If you have heard the word but can't define it:

- Use positive or negative – write a "+" or "–" sign next to the question word and then rule out answer choices that are opposite or neutral
- Use context – in what sentence or phrase have you heard the word before?
- Look for roots and word parts – ask yourself what other words this word looks like

Synonyms practice

Before you answer each question write beside it which strategy you will use from above.

1. FLEXIBLE: Strategy:

   (A) bendable
   (B) illuminated
   (C) supportive
   (D) thorough

2. OMNISCIENT: Strategy:

   (A) all-knowing
   (B) constant
   (C) favorable
   (D) scenic

3. EXCISE: Strategy:

   (A) illuminate
   (B) ponder
   (C) remove
   (D) verify

4. CONFINE: Strategy:

   (A) devote
   (B) incline
   (C) limit
   (D) promote

Sentence Completions strategies

Our basic strategies for sentence completions are:

- First underline the key idea – every sentence completion question has a key idea
- Look for sentences showing contrast and circle any conjunctions that are used to change direction ("however", "but", "although", "even though", "despite")

- Look for sentences showing cause or sequence – these sentences may have the word "because" or words indicating time such as "while" and "after"
- Use our strategies for synonyms when you don't know the meaning of one or more of the answer choices

Sentence Completions practice

1. Since the Arctic Circle is too cold for plants to grow, it is ------- for as far as the eye can see.

   (A) barren
   (B) frigid
   (C) humane
   (D) translucent

2. The writings of John Steinbeck ------- how hard it was for many American citizens during the Great Depression and brought attention to those hardships.

   (A) condensed
   (B) emphasized
   (C) lured
   (D) vanished

3. Artist Claude Monet was inspired by the French countryside and --------.

   (A) traveled frequently
   (B) was born in 1840
   (C) married a woman named Camille
   (D) produced many paintings of natural scenes

Reading Comprehension practice

Reading passage practice

As you work through the passage on the next page, please remember to:

- Mark questions "S" or "G" before you read the passage
- Answer specific questions first and then general questions
- Use ruling out

1   When a natural landscape is destroyed or drastically changed, nature quickly
2   moves in. New plants take root and the habitat grows and changes. The word for this
3   process is succession.

4   Sometimes a new habitat is created when a natural disaster destroys all life in an
5   area. For example, the lava flow from a volcano or mud from a landslide destroys
6   everything in its path. The area is left without any plants. Seeds from plants can float
7   into this area and quickly begin to colonize the bare ground. Without competition from
8   large trees, smaller plants can take root. Gradually, these plants improve the soil in an
9   area and larger plants are able to grow. This is a long and slow process called primary
10   succession.

11   In other situations, large plants and trees are destroyed but smaller plants remain.
12   For example, when a hurricane or tornado disturbs an area, many large plants and trees
13   are destroyed. However, smaller plants and the soil needed for growing larger species
14   remain. Over time, larger plants and trees return to the area. This process is called
15   secondary succession.

16   In both primary and secondary succession, the variety of species continues to grow
17   as plants and trees return to an area. The ecosystem continues to expand until another
18   natural disaster occurs and the cycle of succession begins again.

1. What is the main idea of this passage?

   (A) Animal life follows after plant life returns.
   (B) Ecosystems go through a cycle of regrowth after natural disasters.
   (C) Primary succession takes longer than secondary succession.
   (D) Soil quality determines what type of plants can grow.

2. Which statement about large plants and trees is supported by information in the passage?

   (A) They are more vulnerable than smaller plants during hurricanes.
   (B) They return first after a natural disaster.
   (C) Compared to smaller plants, they better survive landslides.
   (D) They are necessary for the growth of smaller plants.

3. The author implies that large plants and trees are unable to grow over an area destroyed by lava because

   (A) there is not enough sunlight.
   (B) seeds come floating in.
   (C) the soil is not high enough quality.
   (D) smaller plants do not allow larger plants to grow.

4. In line 7, the word "colonize" comes closest in meaning to

   (A) argue.
   (B) destroy.
   (C) glare.
   (D) inhabit.

5. The primary purpose of the last paragraph (lines 16-18) is to

   (A) provide a different opinion.
   (B) introduce a new topic.
   (C) summarize a main idea.
   (D) leave the reader with questions.

Math practice

Quantitative Reasoning and Mathematics Achievement strategies

Answer the questions below about strategy on the math sections:

1. What should we do because this is a multiple-choice test?

2. If there are variables in the answer choices, what should we do?

3. If they ask for the value of a variable, what should we do?

Quantitative Reasoning and Mathematics Achievement practice

1. Which equation correctly shows the associative property?

   (A) $W(X + Y) = WX + WY$
   (B) $(W \times X) \times Y = W \times (X \times Y)$
   (C) $W \times X \times Y = X \times Y \times W$
   (D) $(W - X) - Z = Z - (W - X)$

2. Clarence had two bottles of catsup, neither of which was full. One bottle contained $\frac{2}{3}$ of a cup of catsup and the other bottle contained $\frac{3}{4}$ of a cup of catsup. If he were to combine the content from both bottles, how many total cups of catsup would he have?

   (A) 1

   (B) $1\frac{5}{12}$

   (C) 2

   (D) $2\frac{1}{2}$

3. Pauline was making a necklace. She put 1 red bead on a string, then 2 blue beads, then 3 yellow beads, then 4 black beads. She then started the pattern over by putting 1 red bead on the string and so on. What color will the 18th bead be?

(A) red
(B) blue
(C) yellow
(D) black

4. Isaac received a score of 6 on two quizzes, a score of 8 on another quiz, and a score of 10 on his final quiz. What is the mean score of Isaac's quizzes?

(A) 6
(B) 7
(C) 7.5
(D) 9

5. When it is 9 AM in Boston, it is 7 AM in Denver. A plane leaves Boston at 12 PM and lands in Denver four hours later. What is the time in Denver when the plane lands?

(A) 10 AM
(B) 12 PM
(C) 2 PM
(D) 4 PM

Workout #5 Answers

Vocabulary

Roots questions

1. To *deflect* is to turn something away from you.

2. A *verdict* is what someone believes to be true.

Words to remember questions

1. Essential personnel are employees that are considered so important that they have to come into work, even when everyone else can stay home.

2. A fishing lure is something that fishermen use to attract fish to their hooks. They often look like a type of food that fish like such as insects.

Verbal Reasoning practice

Synonyms practice

1. A is the correct answer choice. The word *flexible* has the *flex* root which means "to bend".

2. A is the correct answer choice. The word *omniscient* has the root *sci* in it which means "to know". It also has the root *omni* in it which means "all".

3. C is the correct answer choice. The word *excise* has two roots – *ex* means "out" and *cis* means "to cut" – so the word *excise* literally means "to cut out". *Remove* comes closest to this meaning.

4. C is the correct answer choice. You might be able to use context on this one – have you ever heard of a dog being confined to part of the house? Or sailors on a ship being in confined quarters? The word *confine* also has two roots – *con* means "with" and *fin* means "end" – so the word means "with endings or limits".

Sentence Completions practice

1. A is the correct answer choice. The word *since* tells us that this is a cause relationship. The cold in the artic would not cause it to be *humane* or *translucent*, so we can rule out choices C and D. Now it is a little trickier. *Frigid* is a tempting answer choice, but the fact that it is too cold for plants to grow doesn't result in it being frigid – it is already frigid. It would result in the land being *barren*, or without anything growing.

2. B is the correct answer choice. As a writer, John Steinbeck would *emphasize*, or show the importance of, how hard it was for Americans during the Great Depression.

3. D is the correct answer. First we have to look at the first part of the sentence. We should underline "French countryside" since that is what the first part of the sentence is talking about. So which answer choice matches most closely with the countryside? Painting natural scenes is the best fit.

Reading Comprehension practice

Reading passage practice

1. B is the correct answer choice. This is a general question so we look to the last sentence for the main idea. Answer choice B best restates the last sentence of the passage.

2. A is the correct answer choice. The passage says that "when a hurricane or tornado disturbs an area, many large plants and trees are destroyed. However, smaller plants and the soil needed for growing larger species remain." This tells us that large plants and trees are more vulnerable because the smaller plants survive.

3. C is the correct answer choice. The second paragraph says about smaller plants that "these plants improve the soil in an area and larger plants are able to grow". This implies that the soil quality right after the disaster is not high enough for larger trees and plants to grow.

4. D is the correct answer choice. For vocabulary in context questions, we go back and cross out the word in the passage and then plug in answer choices. If we cross out the word *colonize* and then put the answer choices in its place, only the word *inhabit* keeps the same meaning for the sentence.

5. C is the correct answer. This is the last paragraph of an informational text, so we would expect that it is summarizing the main idea.

Math practice

Quantitative Reasoning and Mathematics Achievement strategies

1. See if we can estimate before doing long calculations.

2. If there are variables in the answer choices, we should plug in our own numbers.

3. If they ask for the value of a variable, we should plug in answer choices and see what works.

Quantitative Reasoning and Mathematics Achievement practice

1. B is the correct answer choice. The associative property requires a change in groupings, which answer choice B shows. Answer A shows the distributive property and not the associative property, so we can rule out answer choice A. Answer choice C shows the commutative property, so can eliminate that one as well. Answer choice D is not even mathematically correct so it can be ruled out.

2. B is the correct answer choice. In order to add the two fractions, we first need to find a common denominator. Since 3 and 4 both go into 12, that will be our common denominator:

$$\frac{2}{3} + \frac{3}{4} = \frac{8}{12} + \frac{9}{12} = \frac{17}{12} = 1\frac{5}{12}$$

3. D is the correct answer choice. The best way to answer this question is to make a chart showing the colors of each bead:

Bead #	1	2-3	4-6	7-10	11	12-13	14-16	17-20
Color	red	blue	yellow	black	red	blue	yellow	black

From this chart, we can see that the 18th bead will be black.

4. C is the correct answer choice. In order to find the mean, first we have to add up all of the scores. The trick here is to remember that there are TWO scores of 6. The total of Isaac's scores is:

$$6 + 6 + 8 + 10 = 30$$

Now we have to divide this total by the number of scores (4):

$$\frac{30}{4} = 7\frac{1}{2}$$

Answer choice C is correct.

5. C is the correct answer choice. The easiest way to answer this question is to put all of the times into Denver time. If the plane left Boston at 12 PM, then it would have been 10 AM in Denver. Now we can add four hours to that and get that the plane landed at 2 PM Denver time.

Vocabulary

Roots

Below are some roots. I will give you the definition of the root and then two examples of words that have that root. I will give you the definition of each word and then you need to write in an example sentence or a memory trick you will use to remember the meaning of the word. At the end of the roots section, I will ask a question or two that gets you thinking about the roots and their meanings. Then we have the "Words to Remember!" section. These are three words that you need to memorize – I will give you the words and an example sentence, and then you need to answer a question or two about the words.

Be sure to make flashcards (or keep a list) of any words that you don't know. You will be responsible for knowing and applying the definitions of all the roots and words that you have learned as you move through the workouts.

Root: *sens/sent*
Definition – to feel
Examples:
Sensitive – aware of other people's emotions
Sentence or memory trick:

Sensation – a feeling
Sentence or memory trick:

Root: *term*
Definition – to end
Examples:
Terminate – to end
Sentence or memory trick:

Exterminate – the get rid of something completely (such as insects)
Sentence or memory trick:

Roots questions

1. How do you think the root *term* relates to terminals in an airport?

2. What does it mean to lose sensation?

Words to remember!

Elaborate – very detailed
Example: The elaborate plans for the school party were way too complicated.

Objective – based on facts and not opinion
Example: Journalists are supposed to be objective and write articles based on facts and not personal opinions.

Blunder – a careless mistake
Example: It was quite a blunder when the catcher dropped the ball and the opposing team scored a home run.

Words to remember questions

1. Do you think a kitchen or a ballroom would be more elaborately decorated?

2. The opposite of *objective* is *subjective*. What do you think that *subjective* means?

Verbal Reasoning practice

Now that you are more familiar with the strategies, we will skip right to the practice questions. You should try to apply strategy as you work through the practice questions. After you complete the practice, use the strategy checklists to make sure you are developing good habits.

Synonyms practice

1. HUMANE:

   (A) compassionate
   (B) elaborate
   (C) portable
   (D) uniform

2. LURE:

   (A) drench
   (B) export
   (C) report
   (D) tempt

3. CONSCIOUS:

   (A) aware
   (B) objective
   (C) reflective
   (D) verified

4. CONCISE:

   (A) available
   (B) brief
   (C) sensitive
   (D) weary

Synonyms strategies checklist

Check below whether or not you used each strategy.

Did you…	Yes	No
1. Use positive or negative?	___	___
2. Think of where you have heard the word before?	___	___
3. Use roots or word parts?	___	___

Sentence Completions practice

1. It is important that hikers in remote areas carry ------ safety gear such as water, food, and a first aid kit.

   (A) adhesive
   (B) barren
   (C) essential
   (D) translucent

2. Rather than providing a report that was ---------, the journalist was heavily influenced by emotions.

   (A) bloated
   (B) elated
   (C) liberating
   (D) objective

3. When Herman Melville first published Moby Dick it was considered a total failure, but now ----------.

   (A) the book has a whale as a main character
   (B) it is considered a great work of American literature
   (C) it does not sell a lot of copies
   (D) Herman Melville is no longer living

Sentence Completions strategies checklist

Check below whether or not you used each strategy.

Did you...	Yes	No
1. Underline a key word or phrase in EVERY question?	___	___
2. Look for sentences showing a change in direction (and circle the word that shows that contrast)?	___	___
3. Look for sentences showing sequence or cause?	___	___
4. Use our strategies for synonyms if you didn't know one or more of the answer choices?	___	___

Reading Comprehension practice

Reading passage practice

As you work through this passage, please remember to:

- Mark questions "S" or "G" before you read the passage
- Answer specific questions first and then general questions
- Use ruling out

Questions #1-5

1   On a cold and dreary day we set out to canoe through the cold waters of northern
2 Maine. Although it was July, the air temperature was only about fifty degrees. A light
3 drizzle came down on our shoulders as we moved our paddles through the water.
4   We had set out to repair shelters along the Moose River. In one canoe we carried
5 rope, axes, and pieces of canvas. These were the only supplies that we would need to
6 repair the primitive camping tents that dotted the banks of the river.
7   We were not sure what we would find. It had been a long winter in Maine with
8 lots of snow and howling winds. We were not sure how many of the tents, or their
9 platforms, had survived. We had eight miles to paddle before we would make it to the
10 first campsite for the night.
11   The wind blew hard against us. We crouched down as we paddled and kept our
12 heads down. The misty sun was just setting when we came around a bend in the river
13 and spotted the campsite.
14   We pulled our canoe up onto the sandy beach and sat a moment in exhaustion.
15 Slowly, we stood up again and hacked away at the overgrown path that led back to the
16 campsite. We almost cried in relief when we saw that not only was the platform still
17 there, the canvas over it was in perfect condition. We pulled back one flap of the tent
18 and looked inside.
19   On the platform was a neat stack of dry wood. On it was a note that read, "Never
20 forget that the kindness of strangers matters". Whoever the stranger was that left that
21 note, I know that he or she changed the course of at least one life.

1. The primary purpose of this passage is to

   (A) detail how tents are repaired.
   (B) emphasize the importance of dressing properly for outdoor trips.
   (C) share an experience that was important to the narrator.
   (D) describe the geography of northern Maine.

2. In line 6, the word "primitive" most nearly means

   (A) complicated.
   (B) honest.
   (C) miserable.
   (D) simple.

3. Which of the following could be inferred from the last sentence (lines 20-21)?

   (A) The stranger's kind actions influenced the author's life.
   (B) Firewood should be dry in order to be useful.
   (C) Canoeing is hard work.
   (D) The Moose River is in Northern Maine.

4. The author's canoe trip can best be described as

   (A) awkward.
   (B) proper.
   (C) short.
   (D) tiring.

5. In the fourth paragraph (lines 11-13), it is implied that the narrator kept his head down while he paddled because

   (A) he had a long way to paddle that day.
   (B) it was getting dark.
   (C) the wind was blowing strongly.
   (D) the campsite was near.

Math practice

Quantitative Reasoning and Mathematics Achievement strategies

Our basic strategies for the math sections on the ISEE are:

- Estimate – this is a multiple-choice test!
- If there are variables in the answer choices, try plugging in your own numbers
- If they ask for the value of a variable, plug in answer choices

Quantitative Reasoning and Mathematics Achievement practice

1. A certain number can be divided by both 2 and 5 with nothing left over. What other number could this number be divided by with nothing left over?

   (A) 3
   (B) 7
   (C) 8
   (D) 10

2. Which fraction has a value between $\frac{1}{5}$ and $\frac{1}{2}$?

   (A) $\frac{4}{7}$

   (B) $\frac{5}{9}$

   (C) $\frac{6}{11}$

   (D) $\frac{7}{15}$

3. Use the diagram below to answer the question.

If the length of AB is w and the length of AC is v, then which expression would give the length of BC?

(A) $v - w$
(B) $w - v$
(C) $v + w$
(D) $v \times w$

4. Use the Venn Diagram below.

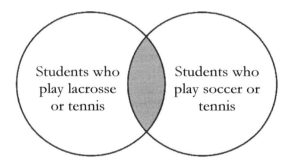

Which of the following students would be found in the shaded region of the Venn Diagram?

(A) a boy who plays lacrosse
(B) a girl who plays tennis
(C) a boy who plays soccer
(D) a girl who plays lacrosse and Frisbee

5. A quadrilateral has vertices at the coordinate points $(3, 1)$, $(2, 4)$, $(3, 7)$, and $(4, 4)$. Which term would best describe this quadrilateral?

(A) square
(B) hexagon
(C) rhombus
(D) trapezoid

Workout #6 Answers

Vocabulary

Roots questions

1. Trips end when the plane parks at the terminal.

2. If you lose sensation, you can no longer feel anything. For example, if you lose sensation in your toes, you cannot feel your toes at all.

Words to remember question

1. A ballroom would be more elaborate since elaborate decorations would be ruined in a working kitchen.

2. Based on emotion and not on facts.

Verbal Reasoning practice

Synonyms practice

1. A is the correct answer choice. If you don't know what the word *compassionate* means, then ruling out would be your best strategy here. *Humane* does not mean complicated (elaborate), able to be carried (portable), or all the same shape or size (uniform). This leaves use with choice A – *compassionate*, or kind and showing sympathy to living creatures. *Humane* is also a word to learn in workout #4 so please study these words if you missed this question.

2. D is the correct answer choice. *Lure* is a word to learn in workout #5 so please study those words if you missed this question.

3. A is the correct answer choice. The word *conscious* has the *sci* root which means "to know". If you are *conscious*, you know what is going on or are aware.

4. B is the correct answer choice. *Concise* has two roots – *con* means "with" and *cis* means "to cut" – so it literally means "with cutting". In actuality, it means that the extra has been cut out so what is left is brief.

Sentence Completions practice

1. C is the correct answer choice. In this question, we have to decide what would describe supplies like water, food, and a first aid kit. These are what you must have to live, so they are *essential*.

2. D is the correct answer choice. The words "rather than" tell us that this is a sentence showing contrast. The second part of the sentence talks about being influenced by emotions, so we know we are looking for a word that means the opposite of being influenced by emotions. *Objective* means sticking to the facts.

3. B is the correct answer choice. This is another sentence showing contrast. The words "but now" tell us that the present condition is different from the past. The beginning of the sentence tells us that Moby Dick was considered a failure so we are looking for an end to the sentence that says the opposite, which answer choice B does.

Reading Comprehension practice

Reading passage practice

1. C is the correct answer choice. This is a narrative passage that describes an event or experience.

2. D is the correct answer choice. This is a vocabulary in context question so we can go back to the passage and cross out the word *primitive* and plug in answer choices in its place. The word *simple* best maintains the meaning of the sentence if we plug it in where *primitive* is.

3. A is the correct answer choice. For this question it is important to stick to that last sentence. The last sentence says that a life was changed and answer choice A repeats this idea. The other answer choices are details that show up in other parts of the passage but not the last sentence.

4. D is the correct answer choice. The author tells us that they "sat a moment in exhaustion" when the trip was over. The word *tiring* repeats the idea of exhaustion.

5. C is the correct answer choice. In the sentence before the comment about keeping their heads down, the author says, "the wind blew hard against us", which implies that they kept their heads down because of the wind.

Math practice

Quantitative Reasoning and Mathematics Achievement practice

1. D is the correct answer. Since the number can be divided by the factors of 10, which are 2 and 5, then it can also be divided by 10 with no remainder.

2. D is the correct answer. This question is actually a great question to use ruling out to answer. If you look at answer choices A-C, those fractions are all clearly greater than one-half. This means that they cannot have a value between $\frac{1}{5}$ and $\frac{1}{2}$. We can see that answer choice D is less than one-half and we don't even have to check to see if it is greater than $\frac{1}{5}$ because it is the only answer choice remaining.

3. A is the correct answer choice. The question gives us the total length and the length of one segment and then asks us for the length of the other segment. In order to find the length of the other segment we would subtract the given segment length (w) from the total (v). Answer choice A correctly represents this.

4. B is the correct answer choice. In order to answer this question, we want to look for the overlap in the two categories. Since a student who plays tennis would show up in both circles, he or she would belong in the shaded region where the two circles overlap. Only answer choice B has a student who plays tennis so that is the correct answer choice.

5. C is the correct answer. The best way to answer this question is to draw out a coordinate graph and plot the points:

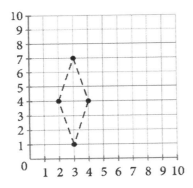

We can see that the figure has four sides of equal length but not four right angles, so the best term for it is rhombus.

Vocabulary

Roots

Below are some roots. I will give you the definition of the root and then two examples of words that have that root. I will give you the definition of each word and then you need to write in an example sentence or a memory trick you will use to remember the meaning of the word. At the end of the roots section, I will ask a question or two that gets you thinking about the roots and their meanings. Then we have the "Words to Remember!" section. These are three words that you need to memorize – I will give you the words and an example sentence, and then you need to answer a question or two about the words.

Be sure to make flashcards (or keep a list) of any words that you don't know. You will be responsible for knowing and applying the definitions of all the roots and words that you have learned as you move through the workouts.

Root: *log*
Definition – word
Examples:
Prologue – introduction
Sentence or memory trick:

Dialogue – conversation between two or more people
Sentence or memory trick:

Root: *merg/mers*
Definition – to dive
Examples:
Submerge – to go under water
Sentence or memory trick:

Immerse – to cover completely with liquid or to become completely involved
Sentence or memory trick:

Roots questions

1. If the root *mono* means "one", what do you think the word *monologue* means?

2. If *submerge* means "to go under water", what do you think the root *sub* means?

Words to remember!

Miser – a very cheap person
Example: Megan was such a miser she would only chew half a piece of gum at a time in order to save money.

Rugged – rough and uneven
Example: You should pack special equipment if you intend to hike in rugged terrain.

Endorse – to support
Example: Many brands of toothpaste claim to be endorsed by dentists so that people will trust the brand.

Words to remember questions

1. Why do you think ads for sport utility vehicles show them driving over rugged ground?

2. Why do political candidates look for endorsements from important people?

Verbal Reasoning practice

Now that you are more familiar with the strategies, we will skip right to the practice questions. You should try to apply strategy as you work through the practice questions. After you complete the practice, use the strategy checklists to make sure you are developing good habits.

Synonyms practice

1. LIBERATE:

   (A) blunder
   (B) decline
   (C) free
   (D) ponder

2. TERMINATE:

   (A) drench
   (B) end
   (C) recline
   (D) submerge

3. ELATED:

   (A) flexible
   (B) illuminated
   (C) overjoyed
   (D) sympathetic

4. BLUNDER:

   (A) duty
   (B) export
   (C) proof
   (D) mistake

Synonyms strategies checklist

Check below whether or not you used each strategy.

Did you…	Yes	No
1. Use positive or negative?	___	___
2. Think of where you have heard the word before?	___	___
3. Use roots or word parts?	___	___

Sentence Completions practice

1. The ------- conditions in the Himalayan Mountains make it almost impossible to cross over them on foot.

   (A) conscious
   (B) essential
   (C) instant
   (D) rugged

2. When planning a party menu it is important to be --------- to the needs of guests who may have food allergies.

   (A) flattering
   (B) hushed
   (C) sensitive
   (D) translucent

3. Although the New Caledonian crested gecko was once considered to be extinct, ---------.

   (A) it was rediscovered in the wreckage of a storm
   (B) it was first described in 1866
   (C) it has crests that run from its eyes to its tail
   (D) it is orange in color

Sentence Completions strategies checklist

Check below whether or not you used each strategy.

Did you…   Yes   No

1. Underline a key word or phrase in EVERY question?   ____   ____

2. Look for sentences showing a change in direction
    (and circle the word that shows that contrast)?   ____   ____

3. Look for sentences showing sequence or cause?   ____   ____

4. Use our strategies for synonyms if you didn't know
    one or more of the answer choices?   ____   ____

Reading Comprehension practice

Reading passage practice

As you work through the passage on the next page, please remember to:

- Mark questions "S" or "G" before you read the passage
- Answer specific questions first and then general questions
- Use ruling out

Questions #1-5

1   Mary Anning was born into a poor family in Lyme Regis, England, in 1799. Lyme
2 Regis a seaside town with cliffs that overlook the ocean. Water would frequently flood
3 these cliffs and wash away soil. When this happened, fossils often emerged from the
4 cliffs. Mary's family had very little money and Mary and her brother would make extra
5 money by uncovering these fossils and selling them to tourists and collectors.

6   When Mary was eleven years old, her brother let her know that a crocodile's
7 skeleton had been partially uncovered in the cliffs. She went and dug out the skull and
8 part of the backbone of the creature. This turned out to be no crocodile, however.
9 Eleven-year-old Mary Anning had uncovered part of an *Ichthyosaurus*, or fish-lizard
10 dinosaur. She sold this find to a collector to help her family pay the bills.

11   Thus began Mary's career as a fossil hunter. Because her family did not have
12 money to pay for schools or books, Mary had very little formal education. She learned
13 what she could by uncovering fossils in the cliffs by her home. She also taught herself
14 about anatomy, paleontology, and geology.

15   She became so respected as a fossil hunter that scientists travelled from as far away
16 as New York City to consult with her and look for fossils together. Her discoveries were
17 some of the most important as scientists tried to piece together what marine life looked
18 like during the Jurassic Period.

1. The primary purpose of this passage is to

   (A) compare Mary Anning and her brother.
   (B) inform the reader about the life of one fossil hunter.
   (C) explain why Mary Anning became a fossil hunter.
   (D) prove the existence of fossils in Lyme Regis, England.

2. In line 3, the word "emerged" comes closest in meaning to

   (A) came out.
   (B) fell off.
   (C) crumbled.
   (D) turned cold.

3. It can be inferred from the second paragraph (lines 6-10) that the skeleton that Mary Anning uncovered was

   (A) a crocodile.
   (B) the very first fossil that she found.
   (C) the first *Ichthyosaurus* found in England.
   (D) something that a collector would be willing to pay money for.

4. The passages implies that Mary Anning was taught primarily by

   (A) teachers at a school.
   (B) her older brother.
   (C) her own discoveries and research.
   (D) other scientists.

5. Which question can be answered with information in the passage?

   (A) Where did Mary Anning live?
   (B) Which scientists came to consult with Mary Anning?
   (C) Which other dinosaur fossils were found in Lyme Regis?
   (D) Why was Mary Anning's family poor?

Math practice

Quantitative Reasoning and Mathematics Achievement strategies

Our basic strategies for the math sections on the ISEE are:

- Estimate – this is a multiple-choice test!
- If there are variables in the answer choices, try plugging in your own numbers
- If they ask for the value of a variable, plug in answer choices

Quantitative Reasoning and Mathematics Achievement practice

1. Vivian's softball team won more than 5 games but less than 9 games. Vivian told a friend that her team won more than 4 games but less than 7 games. How many games did Vivian's softball team win?

    (A) 4
    (B) 5
    (C) 6
    (D) 7

2. Which number is closest to $\frac{1}{3}$ of 43,401?

    (A) 15,023
    (B) 20,450
    (C) 21,980
    (D) 28,954

3. Lowell has a box with red, green, and blue markers in it. There are twice as many green markers as red markers. There are also five times as many blue markers as red markers. If there are a total of 24 markers in the box, then how many of those markers are blue?

    (A) 5
    (B) 10
    (C) 15
    (D) 20

4. A class planted three types of tomato seeds: beefsteak, cherry, and Roma. The plants were placed under a grow lamp so that they each received exactly eight hours of light a day. Each week the class measured the plant growth.

TOMATO PLANT EXPERIMENT

Week	Beefsteak Tomato	Cherry Tomato	Roma Tomato
1	0 inches	1 inch	0 inches
2	2 inches	5 inches	0 inches
3	5 inches	10 inches	2 inches
4	8 inches	16 inches	3 inches
5	10 inches	21 inches	5 inches

If the same pattern of growth continues for the cherry tomato, which could be the predicted height of the cherry tomato plant in week 7?

(A) 25 inches
(B) 30 inches
(C) 36 inches
(D) 40 inches

5. The figure below was created by stacking smaller cubes that each have a volume of 1 cm³.

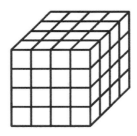

What is the volume of the largest cube?

(A) 4 cm³
(B) 8 cm³
(C) 16 cm³
(D) 64 cm³

Workout #7 Answers

Vocabulary

Roots questions

1. A *monologue* is a speech given by one person.

2. The root *sub* means "under".

Words to remember questions

1. In order to show how tough the sports utility vehicle is.

2. Political candidates are trying to get people to vote for them. If an important person endorses a candidate then other people are likely to vote for that candidate as well.

Verbal Reasoning practice

Synonyms practice

1. C is the correct answer choice. The word *liberate* has the root *lib* which means "to free".

2. B is the correct answer choice. The word *terminate* has the root *term* which means "to end".

3. C is the correct answer choice. This is a word to remember from workout #4 – please review those words if you missed this question.

4. D is the correct answer choice. This is a word to remember from workout #6 – please review these words if you missed this question.

Sentence Completions practice

1. D is the correct answer choice. This is a sentence showing cause. What would make it almost impossible to cross mountains while walking? *Rugged* conditions would. If you didn't remember the meaning of the word *rugged*, please study the words to remember from this workout.

2. C is the correct answer choice. The best strategy for this question is to fill in our own word. If we are trying to plan a party menu, we would want to be aware of the food allergies of our guests. The word *sensitive* is like *aware* so answer choice C is correct.

3. A is the correct answer choice. This is a sentence showing contrast. We would circle the word *although* and underline *extinct*. This tells us that we are looking for an ending for the sentence that is the opposite of *extinct*. Answer choice A offers evidence that the gecko is not really extinct.

Reading Comprehension practice
Reading passage practice

1. B is the correct answer. Answer choices A, C, and D have details mentioned in the passage but are not the primary purpose of the passage. Don't be fooled by the fact that answer choice B does not mention Mary Anning by name. It describes her with the term "fossil hunter" instead.

2. A is the correct answer. This is a vocabulary in context question. To answer this question, we go back to the passage and cross out the word "emerged" in the passage. We then plug in the answer choices in its place and see which one keeps the meaning of the sentence the same. Answer choice A best maintains the meaning of the sentence as a whole.

3. D is the correct answer choice. Answer choices A and C are very tempting because they repeat words from the passage, but the passage does not infer that either total statement is true. The passage does say that a collector bought the partial skeleton, so it must have been something that a collector was willing to pay money for.

4. C is the correct answer choice. The passage tells us that she "learned what she could by uncovering fossils" and "taught herself about anatomy, paleontology, and geology". Answer choice C restates this.

5. A is the correct answer choice. In the very first sentence the passages tells us that she was born in Lyme Regis. Later in the passage, it also references that she still lived by the cliffs.

Math practice

Quantitative Reasoning and Mathematics Achievement practice

1. C is the correct answer choice. If we look at the statement "more than 5 games but less than 9 games", then Vivian's team could have won 6, 7, or 8 games. If you look at the statement, "more than 4 games but less than 7 games", then Vivian's team could have won 5 or 6 games. The only overlap is if Vivian's team won 6 games, so answer choice C is correct.

2. A is the correct answer choice. Since the question asks which number is "closest to" $\frac{1}{3}$ of 43,401 we know that we can round off. If we round off 43,401 to 45,000 then it is easy to find $\frac{1}{3}$ of 45,000. Since 45,000 divided by 3 is 15,000, answer choice A comes closest.

3. C is the correct answer choice. Our first step is to create a ratio. The ratio of red to green to blue markers is $1 : 2 : 5$. Now we have to turn the ratio into fractions that show part out of the whole, instead of comparing parts like our ratio does. In order to create the fractions, we simply add up the "parts" of the ratio to figure out the total parts and make that the bottom of our fractions. Since $1 + 2 + 5 = 8$, we know that $\frac{1}{8}$ of the markers are red, $\frac{2}{8}$ of the markers are green, and $\frac{5}{8}$ of the 24 markers are blue. Since the word "of" tells us to multiply, we can do $\frac{5}{8} \times 24$ in order to find the number of blue markers. The math looks like this:

$$\frac{5}{8} \times 24 = \frac{5}{8} \times \frac{24}{1} = \frac{120}{8} = 15$$

4. B is the correct answer choice. For this question, we need to make sure that we are looking only at the cherry tomato data. We can see that each week the cherry tomato plant grows 4-6 inches. Now we have to remember that they are not asking for the next week but rather how tall the plant will be two weeks from the last week given. This means that we need to add 8-12 inches to the week 5 height. Since the week 5 height was 21 inches, if we add 8-12 inches, we get that the week 7 height should be in the ballpark of 29-33 inches. Only answer choice B falls within that range.

5. D is the correct answer. When we answer this question, we need to remember that there are smaller blocks that make up the larger cube that we cannot see in the picture. We can see that the front face, or "layer" of the cube is made up of 16 smaller blocks. We can also see that there are 4 of these layers going back so we multiply $16 \times 4 = 64$ blocks that make up the larger cube. Since the volume of each smaller cube is 1 cm^3, the volume of the larger cube is 64 cm^3.

Vocabulary

Roots

Below are some roots. I will give you the definition of the root and then two examples of words that have that root. I will give you the definition of each word and then you need to write in an example sentence or a memory trick you will use to remember the meaning of the word. At the end of the roots section, I will ask a question or two that gets you thinking about the roots and their meanings. Then we have the "Words to Remember!" section. These are three words that you need to memorize – I will give you the words and an example sentence, and then you need to answer a question or two about the words.

Be sure to make flashcards (or keep a list) of any words that you don't know. You will be responsible for knowing and applying the definitions of all the roots and words that you have learned as you move through the workouts.

Root: *neg*
Definition – no
Examples:
Negligible – not a large amount
Sentence or memory trick:

Renege – to go back and say no
Sentence or memory trick:

Root: *opt*
Definition – best
Examples:
Optimal – the most desirable
Sentence or memory trick:

Optimist – someone who sees the best in other people or in a situation
Sentence or memory trick:

Roots questions

1. If someone reneges on a promise, what does that mean?

2. What do you think it means to negate what someone says?

Words to remember!

Homely – not attractive
Example: Hairless dogs are quite homely.

Ideal – perfect
Example: The ideal solution for a problem is one that is often not practical.

Brink – edge
Example: You must be very careful when standing on the brink of a cliff.

Words to remember questions

1. What does it mean to be standing on the brink of greatness?

2. Would you rather be homely or ideal?

Verbal Reasoning practice

Now that you are more familiar with the strategies, we will skip right to the practice questions. You should try to apply strategy as you work through the practice questions. After you complete the practice, use the strategy checklists to make sure you are developing good habits.

Synonyms practice

1. SENSATION:

    (A) feeling
    (B) inclination
    (C) term
    (D) vice

2. NEGLIGIBLE:

    (A) elated
    (B) minor
    (C) optimized
    (D) unconscious

3. TERMINATE:

    (A) end
    (B) ponder
    (C) trade
    (D) weigh

4. MONOLOGUE:

    (A) lure
    (B) portal
    (C) race
    (D) speech

Synonyms strategies checklist

Check below whether or not you used each strategy.

Did you…	Yes	No
1. Use positive or negative?	___	___
2. Think of where you have heard the word before?	___	___
3. Use roots or word parts?	___	___

Sentence Completions practice

1. Carrie was a genuine ------- who always believed that the something good was about to happen.

   (A) blunder
   (B) miser
   (C) optimist
   (D) scholar

2. Benjamin Franklin is famous for being a(n) -------- who refused to spend any more money than absolutely necessary.

   (A) exterminator
   (B) liberator
   (C) miser
   (D) traveler

3. Although many Americans have never heard of the Louisiana Purchase, it is an event that ---------.

   (A) wasn't all that important
   (B) played a large part in the development of America
   (C) was brought about by Thomas Jefferson
   (D) cost very little money

Sentence Completions strategies checklist

Check below whether or not you used each strategy.

Did you...   Yes   No

1. Underline a key word or phrase in EVERY question?   ____   ____

2. Look for sentences showing a change in direction
   (and circle the word that shows that contrast)?   ____   ____

3. Look for sentences showing sequence or cause?   ____   ____

4. Use our strategies for synonyms if you didn't know
   one or more of the answer choices?   ____   ____

Reading Comprehension practice

Reading passage practice

As you work through this passage, please remember to:

- Mark questions "S" or "G" before you read the passage
- Answer specific questions first and then general questions
- Use ruling out

Questions #1-5

1   In America, most schools have a schedule that includes a long summer break. This
2 schedule was originally developed when most Americans were farmers. Children
3 needed to help out on family farms during the summer so the school calendar was
4 arranged around the growing season.

5   America has changed as a country, though. Now, a very small percentage of
6 students are from families that farm. Also, farming is now done with large machines
7 and not the labor of school-aged children. Many have begun to question whether or not
8 our students still need a long summer break. Some of these people have suggested that
9 schools should operate all year long.

10   While the summer break is no longer necessary for farming, it would be a mistake
11 to take it away. There are many opportunities that American children only have during
12 the summer months. They attend camp and pursue interests that are not taught in
13 textbooks. Without an extended summer break, this would not be possible.

14   Also, there is an epidemic of childhood obesity in America. Many students are
15 now overweight partially because American children are no longer as active as they used
16 to be. The more hours that students spend behind a desk, the less time they have to run
17 around outside and be physically active. The summer provides the best weather for this
18 kind of activity. Moving to year-round school means that students would no longer
19 have extended periods of time to be active while the weather is good.

20   Finally, the summer break is important for teachers. The summer break gives them
21 time to recharge after a stressful year. It also gives them time to attend teaching trainings
22 and think about changes to their own curriculum and materials. Teachers return to the
23 classroom after a summer break ready to bring enthusiasm to their classrooms.

1. The main purpose of this passage is to

   (A) describe why American students have a summer break.
   (B) convince the reader that a long summer break is the best decision for American schools.
   (C) explain one cause of childhood obesity.
   (D) prove that year-round school is effective.

2. According to the passage, what is one reason that some people support year-round schooling?

   (A) Children are no longer needed to work on farms in the summer.
   (B) Teachers need a long summer break to regain their energy and enthusiasm.
   (C) Childhood obesity will be helped by year-round schooling.
   (D) Many working parents support year-round schooling.

3. In the fourth paragraph (lines 14-19), the author implies that if students were in school during the summer

   (A) farms would suffer.
   (B) teachers would be more relaxed.
   (C) student grades would be better.
   (D) they would be less physically active than if they were not in school.

4. According to the passage, why did the long summer break initially come about?

   (A) Teachers were needed to work on farms.
   (B) Students had to travel a long distance to get to school.
   (C) School-aged children often worked in fields during the summer.
   (D) Teachers needed the break to attend teacher trainings.

5. The function of the last paragraph (lines 20-23) is to

   (A) provide evidence that supports the main argument.
   (B) suggest an alternate viewpoint.
   (C) describe one situation.
   (D) summarize the passage.

Math practice

Quantitative Reasoning and Mathematics Achievement strategies

Our basic strategies for the math sections on the ISEE are:

- Estimate – this is a multiple-choice test!
- If there are variables in the answer choices, try plugging in your own numbers
- If they ask for the value of a variable, plug in answer choices

Quantitative Reasoning and Mathematics Achievement practice

1. Which is equal to $403 - 87$?

   (A) 316
   (B) 326
   (C) 330
   (D) 336

2. Use the number line below.

   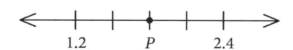

   What number does point P represent?

   (A) 1.4
   (B) 1.5
   (C) 1.8
   (D) 2.0

3. Milton bought 3 packs of gum that cost $2 each and a gallon of milk. If his total (before tax) was $11, then which equation will allow Milton to find the cost of a gallon of milk (m)?

   (A) $2 + m = 11$
   (B) $3 + m = 11$
   (C) $3(2) + 3m = 11$
   (D) $3(2) + m = 11$

4. A poll was taken asking people what their favorite day of the week is. The results are below.

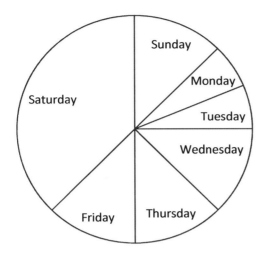

If **10,000** people chose Wednesday as their favorite day, then how many people chose Saturday as their favorite day?

(A) 10,000
(B) 30,000
(C) 40,000
(D) 80,000

5. What is the best name for a parallelogram that has four equal sides and four right angles?

(A) right triangle
(B) trapezoid
(C) square
(D) hexagon

Workout #8 Answers

Vocabulary

Roots questions

1. It means that he or she goes back on a promise.

2. If you negate what someone said it means that you provide evidence that it is wrong.

Words to remember questions

1. It means that greatness is right around the corner for you. Success is about to happen.

2. It depends – would you rather be perfect or unattractive? Most people would prefer to be ideal.

Verbal Reasoning practice

Synonyms practice

1. A is the correct answer choice. The word *sensation* has the root *sens* which means "to feel".

2. B is the correct answer. The *neg* root means "no" and *negligible* means "not a lot" or "minor".

3. A is the correct answer choice. The *term* root means "to end".

4. D is the correct answer. The word *monologue* has two roots – *mono* means "one" and *log* means "word" – so *monologue* is literally words by one person, or a speech.

Sentence Completions practice

1. C is the correct answer. The *opt* root means "best" and an *optimist* is a person who believes that the best will happen.

2. C is the correct answer. A *miser* is a person who is cheap. *Miser* is a word to remember from workout #7 so please review those words if you missed this question.

3. B is the correct answer choice. This is a sentence showing contrast. You should have circled "although" and underlined "never heard of". We are looking for an answer choice that would contrast with the fact that many Americans have not heard of the Louisiana Purchase. Answer choice B tells us that it was very important so it is the best answer choice.

Reading Comprehension practice

Reading passage practice

1. B is the correct answer choice. This is a persuasive passage designed to convince the reader that a summer break is necessary. Answer choices A and C are details from the passage but not the primary purpose. Answer choice D states the opposite of what the passage is trying to accomplish.

2. A is the correct answer choice. Answer choice B actually supports why schools should NOT have a year-round schedule. The passage says the opposite of choice C. Answer choice D is simply not mentioned in the passage. The passage does provide evidence that children are no longer needed on farms, which has led some to question the necessity of a long summer break.

3. D is the correct answer. In the fourth paragraph, the author tells us that childhood obesity is a problem and that a long summer break allows students to be more active in the summer. This makes the assumption that if they are in school during the summer they would be less active.

4. C is the correct answer choice. Answer choice A is tempting because it does mention someone working on farms, but the passage tells us it was the students and not the teachers. Answer choice D is also tempting because the passage argues that teachers now need the break for teacher trainings, but that is not why the break was initially put into the schedule.

5. A is the correct answer choice. This is a persuasive passage making the argument that schools should keep a long summer break. The fifth paragraph provides evidence for this argument.

Math practice

Quantitative Reasoning and Mathematics Achievement practice

1. A is the correct answer choice. If you missed this one, go back and make sure that you borrowed correctly.

2. C is the correct answer choice. With number line questions, we often have to use the points given in order to determine the scale. In this case, there are 4 segments between 1.2 and 2.4. That means that the number line must be counting by 0.3. If we start at 1.2, then the next dash represents 1.5. The following dash, or point P, represents 1.8.

3. D is the correct answer choice. In order to answer this question, let's think about how we would find the total if it was not given. We would take the cost of the gum ($2) and multiply it by 3 since he bought three packs of gum. Then we would add the cost of the milk in order to figure out the total. Answer choice D correctly represents this.

4. B is the correct answer choice. The best way to answer this question is to compare the Wednesday section of the graph to the Saturday section of the circle. The Wednesday section takes up about $\frac{1}{8}$ of the circle and the Saturday section takes up about $\frac{3}{8}$ of the circle. Since $\frac{1}{8} \times 3 = \frac{3}{8}$, we can multiply the number of people who preferred Wednesday (10,000) by 3 and get that 30,000 people preferred Saturday.

5. C is the correct answer choice. A parallelogram by definition has four sides, so we can rule out answer choices A and D because these shapes do not have four sides. The question also tells us that the shape has four right angles, so we can rule out choice B since a trapezoid does not have four right angles. A square does have four sides of equal length and four right angles.

Vocabulary

Roots

Below are some roots. I will give you the definition of the root and then two examples of words that have that root. I will give you the definition of each word and then you need to write in an example sentence or a memory trick you will use to remember the meaning of the word. At the end of the roots section, I will ask a question or two that gets you thinking about the roots and their meanings. Then we have the "Words to Remember!" section. These are three words that you need to memorize – I will give you the words and an example sentence, and then you need to answer a question or two about the words.

Be sure to make flashcards (or keep a list) of any words that you don't know. You will be responsible for knowing and applying the definitions of all the roots and words that you have learned as you move through the workouts.

Root: *reg*
Definition – to rule
Examples:
Regal – characteristic of a king or queen
Sentence or memory trick:

Regulate – to control or rule
Sentence or memory trick:

Root: *mim*
Definition – same
Examples:
Mimic – to imitate or copy
Sentence or memory trick:

Pantomime – to act out or copy a gesture (pretend to be doing something)
Sentence or memory trick:

Roots question

1. What do you think a *regime* is?

Words to remember!

Calamity – a disaster
Example: It was a calamity when Hurricane Sandy flooded towns along the New Jersey coast.

Consent – permission
Example: You need to get your parent's consent before going on the fieldtrip.

Thorough – complete
Example: After a thorough search of the sofa pillows we were sure that the car keys had not been lost there.

Words to remember questions

1. Can you think of an example of a calamity?

2. When you are cleaning the kitchen why do you need to be thorough?

Verbal Reasoning practice

Now that you are more familiar with the strategies, we will skip right to the practice questions. You should try to apply strategy as you work through the practice questions. After you complete the practice, use the strategy checklists to make sure you are developing good habits.

Synonyms practice

1. CONSCIOUS:

   (A) aware
   (B) flexible
   (C) quaint
   (D) supportive

2. VERIFY:

   (A) adhere
   (B) confirm
   (C) decline
   (D) treat

3. IMMERSE:

   (A) admit
   (B) break
   (C) cover
   (D) lure

4. HOMELY:

   (A) elated
   (B) hoarse
   (C) sensitive
   (D) unattractive

Synonyms strategies checklist

Check below whether or not you used each strategy.

Did you…	Yes	No
1. Use positive or negative?	___	___
2. Think of where you have heard the word before?	___	___
3. Use roots or word parts?	___	___

Sentence Completions practice

1. Many Americans lost money in the banking panic in 1907 which led to demands for laws that would better -------- the activity of banks.

   (A) endorse
   (B) mimic
   (C) regulate
   (D) spread

2. Scientists are able to produce sounds that ------- the noises that dolphins make so that they can "talk" to the dolphins.

   (A) consent
   (B) mimic
   (C) push
   (D) terminate

3. Composer George Gershwin started his career by writing short songs for the radio but eventually worked up to ----------.

   (A) composing full length operas
   (B) living in Los Angeles
   (C) enjoying classical concerts
   (D) learning to play the piano

Sentence Completions strategies checklist

Check below whether or not you used each strategy.

Did you...   Yes   No

1. Underline a key word or phrase in EVERY question?   ___   ___

2. Look for sentences showing a change in direction
   (and circle the word that shows that contrast)?   ___   ___

3. Look for sentences showing sequence or cause?   ___   ___

4. Use our strategies for synonyms if you didn't know
   one or more of the answer choices?   ___   ___

Reading Comprehension practice

Reading passage practice

As you work through the passage on the following page, please remember to:

- Mark questions "S" or "G" before you read the passage
- Answer specific questions first and then general questions
- Use ruling out

Questions #1-5

1   Almost as long as there have been humans, people have been bowling in one form
2 or another. In the 1930s, Sir Flinders Petrie discovered objects in a grave from ancient
3 Egypt that appeared to be used for bowling. This would make the sport of bowling over
4 3,000 years old. While there are many forms of bowling, the basic idea is really quite
5 simple – a person rolls a ball at a target.
6   There is also evidence that throughout history bowling was seen as a source of
7 concern. In 1366, King Edward III banned bowling. He was concerned that bowling
8 was distracting his troops from more important activities. He wanted his soldiers
9 practicing their archery skills and not bowling. In the United States, in 1841 the state of
10 Connecticut outlawed "any ninepin lanes". This was an attempt to prevent the
11 gambling that often went along with bowling.
12   Bowling was a sport that was becoming increasingly popular, however. In the early
13 twentieth century many very wealthy families installed bowling alleys in their
14 basements. It was considered a symbol of achievement if you could afford a bowling
15 alley in your home.
16   Perhaps the most important development in the sport of bowling occurred in 1951.
17 This is when the American Machine and Foundry Company (AMF) purchased the
18 patent for a machine that automatically sets up the pins that are knocked down. Before
19 this machine, a "pinboy" had to be employed. After a player took a turn, the pinboy
20 would have to stand all the pins back up for the next player. With the invention of the
21 automatic pin resetting machine, the popularity of bowling exploded.
     The Professional Bowlers Association was formed and major networks began
22 broadcasting bowling tournaments. In 1961, the American Broadcasting Corporation
23 (ABC) was the first network to show a competition of the Professional Bowlers
24 Association on television. Bowling had finally arrived.

1. Which best describes the main idea of this passage?

   (A) Early bowlers would not recognize the sport today.
   (B) Bowling is often linked to gambling.
   (C) ABC was the first network to air bowling tournaments.
   (D) Bowling is a sport that has grown in popularity.

2. The third paragraph (lines 12-15) implies that bowling alleys were

   (A) expensive to build.
   (B) found in ancient Egypt.
   (C) banned by Edward III.
   (D) often a source of annoyance.

3. By saying, "Bowling had finally arrived," the author is suggesting that bowling

   (A) is still relatively unknown.
   (B) had become respected as a sport.
   (C) was commonly associated with gambling.
   (D) was limited by the use of pinboys.

4. In the fourth paragraph, the author says "the popularity of bowling exploded" (line 21) for what reason?

   (A) The game was changed to make the scoring easier.
   (B) Bowling was promoted by soldiers.
   (C) The invention of pin resetting machines meant that bowling alleys no longer needed to employ pinboys.
   (D) Wealthy families had bowling alleys in their basements.

5. The author's tone in the passage can best be described as

   (A) angry.
   (B) bored.
   (C) excited.
   (D) informative.

Math practice

Quantitative Reasoning and Mathematics Achievement strategies

Our basic strategies for the math sections on the ISEE are:
- Estimate – this is a multiple-choice test!
- If there are variables in the answer choices, try plugging in your own numbers
- If they ask for the value of a variable, plug in answer choices

Quantitative Reasoning and Mathematics Achievement practice

1. Use the given number line to answer the question.

   The point Q represents what number?

   (A) 64
   (B) 66
   (C) 68
   (D) 69

2. There are 45 students in Mr. Arnold's class. If 23 of those students returned their books on library day, about what percent of his class did not return their books?

   (A) 10%
   (B) 25%
   (C) 50%
   (D) 70%

3. If ■ + (3 × 4) = 24, then what is the value of ■?

   (A) 2
   (B) 3
   (C) 4
   (D) 12

4. The table below shows the average high temperatures for three weeks in degrees Fahrenheit.

Week	Monday	Tuesday	Wednesday	Thursday	Friday	Saturday	Sunday
1	80	78	85	81	78	90	86
2	85	80	87	80	79	82	88
3	79	82	87	88	90	84	81

What is the mode of the data in this table?

(A) 80
(B) 82
(C) 85
(D) 90

5. If the perimeter of rhombus is $12w$, then what is the length of one side of that rhombus?

(A) 3
(B) 4
(C) $3w$
(D) $4w$

Workout #9 Answers

Vocabulary

Roots question

1. A regime is a government that rules a country. It generally refers to a government that is not elected by the citizens.

Words to remember questions

1. Answers will vary – any disaster would be an example of a calamity.

2. You need to be thorough when you clean a kitchen in order to make sure you kill all the germs that could make your family sick.

Verbal Reasoning practice

Synonyms practice

1. A is the correct answer choice. The word *conscious* contains the root *sci* which means "to know". Answer choice A comes closest to this meaning.

2. B is the correct answer choice. The root *ver* means "truth" so to *verify* means "to find out if something is true, or confirm it".

3. C is the correct answer choice. The word *immerse* has the root *mers* which means "to dive". To *immerse* something is to completely surround or cover something with water. For example, you might immerse a dirty dish in a sink full of water.

4. D is the correct answer choice. *Homely* is a word to remember from workout #8 so please review these words if you missed this question.

Sentence Completions practice

1. C is the correct answer choice. This sentence has a cause relationship. If a lot of people lost money, what would they want to happen to banking activities? They would want them better controlled. The *reg* root means "to rule", so *regulate* means "to add or enforce rules", which is what people who lost money would want.

2. B is the correct answer choice. *Mimic* has the *mim* root that means "same". Scientists would want to make the same noises as the dolphins in order to "talk" with them.

3. A is the correct answer choice. This is a sequence sentence. The beginning of the sentence tells us that he wrote short songs and then he worked up to whatever is in the blank. So what would be the next step in the progression from writing short songs? Answer choice A works – writing full length operas could be the next step in the progression.

Reading Comprehension practice

Reading passage practice

1. D is the correct answer choice. For general questions, we can look to the last sentence. The last sentence tells us that "bowling had finally arrived" and answer choice D restates this idea. Answer choice A has no evidence in the passage and answer choices B and C provide details but are not the main idea.

2. A is the correct answer choice. The third paragraph tells us that wealthy families built them as "a symbol of achievement if you could afford a bowling alley in your home". This implies that most people could not afford to build a bowling alley.

3. B is the correct answer choice. Earlier in the same paragraph, the author discusses how a professional bowling group had formed and a television network started airing bowling tournaments. This suggests that it had become a respected sport.

4. C is the correct answer choice. In the beginning of the same sentence the author discusses the invention of the pin resetting machine, so it is a logical conclusion that the popularity of bowling was linked to this new machine.

5. D is the correct answer choice. This is a nonfiction piece about the history of bowling. Answer choices A, B, and C are too emotional for a nonfiction piece.

Math practice

Quantitative Reasoning and Mathematics Achievement practice

1. B is the correct answer choice. Our first step is to use the two points given (70 and 80) to figure out what the number line is counting by. The difference between 70 and 80 is 10 but there are only 5 segments, so we know the number line must be counting by 2. Now we have to count back from 70 to figure out the value of point Q. The dash to the left of the 70 represents 68, and then the next dash to the left (point Q) represents 66.

2. C is the correct answer choice. The number 23 is about half of 45 and if we use equivalent fractions, we can see that $\frac{1 \times 50}{2 \times 50} = \frac{50}{100}$ or 50%. If 50% returned their books, then 50% did not return their books.

3. D is the correct answer. In order to answer this question we have to remember to follow order of operations, or PEMDAS. If we do what is in the parentheses first, we get ■ + 12 = 24 and ■ must be equal to 12.

4. A is the correct answer choice. The mode is the number that shows up most frequently in a set of data. The best way to answer this question is to systematically count how many data points we have for each number:

Data point	Frequency
78	II
79	II
80	III
81	II
82	II
84	I
85	II
86	I
87	II
88	II
90	II

From this chart, we can clearly see that 80 shows up most often, so that is our mode.

5. C is the correct answer. A rhombus has four sides that are all the same length, so we can simply divide the perimeter ($12w$) by 4 and get that the length of each side is $3w$. It is very easy on this question to forget about the w so watch out for that.

Vocabulary

Roots

Below are some roots. I will give you the definition of the root and then two examples of words that have that root. I will give you the definition of each word and then you need to write in an example sentence or a memory trick you will use to remember the meaning of the word. At the end of the roots section, I will ask a question or two that gets you thinking about the roots and their meanings. Then we have the "Words to Remember!" section. These are three words that you need to memorize – I will give you the words and an example sentence, and then you need to answer a question or two about the words.

Be sure to make flashcards (or keep a list) of any words that you don't know. You will be responsible for knowing and applying the definitions of all the roots and words that you have learned as you move through the workouts.

Root: *tract*
Definition – to pull
Examples:
Attract – to pull something toward another thing
Sentence or memory trick:

Contract – to pull in
Sentence or memory trick:

Root: *rupt*
Definition – to break
Examples:
Rupture – to break
Sentence or memory trick:

Erupt – to burst out
Sentence or memory trick:

Roots questions

1. How is the word *tractor* related to the *tract* root?

2. How is the word *interrupt* related to the *rupt* root?

Words to remember!

Meddle – to interfere in an unwanted way
Example: Edna has a bad habit of listening in on conversations and then meddling in other people's affairs.

Favorable – positive or offering an advantage
Example: The winds were favorable and our boat trip across the bay was faster than we expected.

Devotion – dedication or attachment to a person or task
Example: Verna showed great devotion when she went to her grandmother's house every day to read to her.

Words to remember questions

1. What do you think happens when a person *meddles* in another person's business?

2. If you were planning on having a birthday party outside, would it be *favorable* if it rained?

Verbal Reasoning practice

Now that you are more familiar with the strategies, we will skip right to the practice questions. You should try to apply strategy as you work through the practice questions. After you complete the practice, use the strategy checklists to make sure you are developing good habits.

Synonyms practice

1. OPTIMAL:

   (A) best
   (B) cooperative
   (C) submerged
   (D) thorough

2. MIMIC:

   (A) devote
   (B) emphasize
   (C) imitate
   (D) ponder

3. EXTRACT:

   (A) consult
   (B) deflect
   (C) post
   (D) remove

4. CALAMITY:

   (A) brink
   (B) disaster
   (C) pantomime
   (D) resistance

Synonyms strategies checklist

Check below whether or not you used each strategy.

Did you…	Yes	No
1. Use positive or negative?	___	___
2. Think of where you have heard the word before?	___	___
3. Use roots or word parts?	___	___

Sentence Completions practice

1. Be careful not to place your glass on the -------- of the table because it might fall off and break.

   (A) brink
   (B) folly
   (C) image
   (D) receipt

2. The Trojan Horse was a(n) --------- war strategy that took a lot of planning and coordination.

   (A) concise
   (B) elaborate
   (C) rugged
   (D) typical

3. Unlike Samuel, who became excited very easily, Grant --------.

   (A) often was late to class
   (B) was the first in line most of the time
   (C) was not easily impressed
   (D) studied late into the night

Sentence Completions strategies checklist

Check below whether or not you used each strategy.

Did you…	Yes	No
1. Underline a key word or phrase in EVERY question?	___	___
2. Look for sentences showing a change in direction (and circle the word that shows that contrast)?	___	___
3. Look for sentences showing sequence or cause?	___	___
4. Use our strategies for synonyms if you didn't know one or more of the answer choices?	___	___

Reading Comprehension practice

Reading passage practice

As you work through this passage, please remember to:

- Mark questions "S" or "G" before you read the passage
- Answer specific questions first and then general questions
- Use ruling out

Questions #1-5

1   One cold fall day I got a call from my elderly aunt. She lived across town in an old,
2 rickety house. She had decided that her attic needed to be cleaned out and that it needed
3 to be done that day. She had also decided that I was going to be her helper.

4   With a grumble, I bundled up in warm clothes and trudged across town. My aunt
5 answered the door and led me up the narrow stairway. It was dimly lit and there were
6 cobwebs growing in the corners. I didn't bother taking my coat off since I figured it
7 would be freezing in the unheated attic.

8   My aunt pushed open the creaky door to the attic room and groped in the dark for
9 the pull chain that would turn on the light. When the light came on, I gasped in surprise.
10 Rather than being a dusty old attic, the room was a treasure trove of goods collected
11 throughout my aunt's eccentric life.

12   There was a little trapdoor in the chimney that my aunt had opened and the space
13 was pleasantly warm. I peeled off my many layers and my aunt and I settled into a plush
14 antique sofa. She told me that she had bought it at a market in Paris many years ago.

15   It dawned on me that she didn't want a companion for cleaning. She wanted
16 someone to walk down memory lane with her. She sat down next to me and started to
17 flip through an old photo album. She told me fascinating tales of all the places she had
18 travelled around the world.

19   As the afternoon wore on, we sorted through old trunks of clothing. She pulled on
20 a glamorous straw hat from her days of sunbathing on foreign beaches. She wrapped
21 me up in a fur coat and insisted that I try on her best pearls. The afternoon wore on and
22 the sun sunk lower on the horizon, but in my aunt's attic, the lights just seemed to shine
23 brighter.

1. This passage is mainly concerned with describing

    (A) the weather on a fall day.
    (B) problems with old houses.
    (C) the value of collectables.
    (D) time that the narrator spent with a relative.

2. In line 4, the word "trudged" comes closest in meaning to

    (A) spoke enthusiastically.
    (B) stayed home.
    (C) walked reluctantly.
    (D) wrote slowly.

3. By the end of the passage the author seems to have

    (A) changed her mind about spending time with her aunt.
    (B) finished cleaning out her aunt's attic.
    (C) returned home.
    (D) decided to travel to Paris.

4. Which question could be answered with information from the passage?

    (A) What town did the author live in?
    (B) In what season did this story take place?
    (C) What was the name of the author's aunt?
    (D) How many years old was the author's aunt?

5. When the author says, "It dawned on me" in line 15, what does the author mean by that expression?

    (A) The sun was coming up.
    (B) A thought occurred to the author.
    (C) The author started to clean.
    (D) The author's aunt was starting to get bored.

Math practice

Quantitative Reasoning and Mathematics Achievement strategies

Our basic strategies for the math sections on the ISEE are:

- Estimate – this is a multiple-choice test!
- If there are variables in the answer choices, try plugging in your own numbers
- If they ask for the value of a variable, plug in answer choices

Quantitative Reasoning and Mathematics Achievement practice

1. Which number could be divided by 6 without leaving a remainder?

   (A) 202
   (B) 203
   (C) 204
   (D) 206

2. What is the value of $2.4 + 3.2$?

   (A) $4\dfrac{3}{5}$

   (B) $4\dfrac{4}{5}$

   (C) $5\dfrac{1}{5}$

   (D) $5\dfrac{3}{5}$

3. Use the sequence below in order to answer the question.

$$1,2,4,7,11,16,\_\_\_$$

Which number should replace the _____ in the sequence?

(A) 20
(B) 22
(C) 24
(D) 26

4. Deanne has a box filled with yellow, green, blue, and black pencils. If the probability of randomly picking a green pencil is 3 in 7, then which combination of pencils would be possible?

(A) 9 green pencils and 12 other pencils
(B) 9 green pencils and 21 other pencils
(C) 12 green pencils and 10 other pencils
(D) 15 green pencils and 24 other pencils

5. Use the figure below to answer the question.

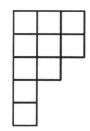

Which piece would complete the figure to make a rectangle?

(A)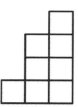

(B)

(C)

(D)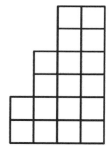

Workout #10 Answers

Vocabulary

Roots questions

1. A *tractor* is a machine that is used to pull farm equipment.

2. When you *interrupt*, you break into someone else's conversation.

Words to remember questions

1. The other person generally gets annoyed or angry.

2. No! It would not be to your advantage if it rained during your outdoor party.

Verbal Reasoning practice

Synonyms practice

1. A is the correct answer choice. *Optimal* has the root *opt* which means "best".

2. C is the correct answer choice. *Mimic* has the root *mim* which means "same". *Imitate* is to act the same as someone else.

3. D is the correct answer choice. *Extract* has two roots – *ex* means "out" and *tract* means "to pull" – so the word literally means "to pull out". Remove comes closest to this meaning.

4. B is the correct answer. This is a word to remember from workout #9 so please review those words if you missed this question.

Sentence Completions practice

1. A is the correct answer choice. The *brink* is the edge of the table. If you didn't know the meaning of this word, please study the words to remember from workout #8.

2. B is the correct answer choice. In this sentence we would underline "a lot of planning and coordination" since that describes what this type of strategy would require. An *elaborate* strategy would require planning and coordination.

3. C is the correct answer choice. This is a sentence showing contrast. The word *unlike* tells us that Grant is the opposite of someone who is easily excited. Answer choice C comes closest.

Reading Comprehension practice

Reading passage practice

1. D is the correct answer choice. This is a narrative passage concerned with the describing the interaction between two people. Don't be fooled by answer choices A and B – they provide details from the passage but are not what the passage is mainly concerned with.

2. C is the correct answer choice. This is a vocabulary in context question so we go back to the passage and cross out the word "trudged" and fill in the answer choices in its place. Earlier in the sentence the author says that she bundled up "with a grumble", which goes along with walking reluctantly.

3. A is the correct answer. At the beginning of the passage the author is not at all excited about going to her aunt's house. By the end, however, the author appears to be having a good time and answer choice A reflects this change.

4. B is the correct answer choice. In the first sentence the author says "one cold fall day". For this type of question, the answer can often be found in just a word or two. The trick is being able to find that word or two quickly.

5. B is the correct answer. If you go back to the sentence you can see that the author had a new thought and figured out her aunt's real motivation. Answer choice B best reflects this.

Math practice

Quantitative Reasoning and Mathematics Achievement practice

1. C is the correct answer choice. A number is divisible by 6 if it is divisible by both 2 and 3. Answer choice B is an odd number so it is not divisible by 2 and we can rule it out. If a number is divisible by 3 then the digits added together will be divisible by 3. If we add the digits for answer choice A, we get $2 + 0 + 2 = 4$. Since 4 is not divisible by 3, we can rule out choice A. Now let's try choice C (we have already ruled out choice B). If we add the digits for choice C, we get $2 + 0 + 4 = 6$. Since 6 is divisible by 3, answer choice C is correct.

2. D is the correct answer choice. This problem is a little trickier. We have to add the numbers first: $2.4 + 3.2 = 5.6$. Now if we look at the answer choices, we see that we have to convert this into a mixed number in order to choose the correct answer. We can use place value to do this: $5.6 = 5\frac{6}{10}$. Now we have to reduce $\frac{6}{10}$ and get a final answer of $5\frac{3}{5}$.

3. B is the correct answer choice. Our first step in answering this question is to figure out the pattern for the sequence. The difference between the first two numbers is 1, the difference between the second and third numbers is 2, the difference between the third and fourth numbers is 3. If we continue this pattern, we can see that we would need to add 6 to 16 in order to get the next number in the sequence. Since $16 + 6 = 22$, we know that answer choice B is correct.

4. A is the correct answer choice. This is a very tricky question! The key to this question is to recognize that the probability gives part to whole (i.e., out of a total of 7 pencils, 3 of them are green), but the answer choices give part to part. We need to convert our probability into part to part: for every 3 green pencils there will be 4 other pencils. Now we look for the answer choice that has that same ratio. With answer choice A, we multiply 3 by 3 to get 9 and we multiply 4 by 3 to get 12. Since we multiplied both parts of our ratio by the same number, choice A works.

5. A is the correct answer choice. The best way to approach this question is to draw each answer choice into the question figure. If you do this, you can see that choice A fits together with the question picture to create a rectangle.

Vocabulary

Roots

Below are some roots. I will give you the definition of the root and then two examples of words that have that root. I will give you the definition of each word and then you need to write in an example sentence or a memory trick you will use to remember the meaning of the word. At the end of the roots section, I will ask a question or two that gets you thinking about the roots and their meanings. Then we have the "Words to Remember!" section. These are three words that you need to memorize – I will give you the words and an example sentence, and then you need to answer a question or two about the words.

Be sure to make flashcards (or keep a list) of any words that you don't know. You will be responsible for knowing and applying the definitions of all the roots and words that you have learned as you move through the workouts.

Root: *migr*
Definition – to change or move
Examples:
Migrate – to change location
Sentence or memory trick:

Immigrate – to move into a country
Sentence or memory trick:

Root: *ques/quir/quis*
Definition – to ask
Examples:
Inquire – to ask about
Sentence or memory trick:

Request – to ask for something
Sentence or memory trick:

Roots questions

1. If *immigrate* means "to move into a country", what do you think *emigrate* means?

2. Can you think of any other words with the *ques/quis/quir* root?

Words to remember!

Foster – to encourage
Example: Thelma has really fostered a love for the arts with her son by taking him to museums and art shows frequently.

Pacify – to make calm or peaceful
Example: Bank tellers often give children lollipops in order to pacify them while they are at the bank.

Prim – proper
Example: It is very easy to offend a prim person.

Words to remember questions

1. Why do you think we give a baby a pacifier?

2. Can you think of a character in a book who is very prim?

Verbal Reasoning practice

Now that you are more familiar with the strategies, we will skip right to the practice questions. You should try to apply strategy as you work through the practice questions. After you complete the practice, use the strategy checklists to make sure you are developing good habits.

Synonyms practice

1. REGAL:

    (A) frigid
    (B) inventive
    (C) kingly
    (D) sympathetic

2. MEDDLE:

    (A) drench
    (B) interfere
    (C) mimic
    (D) renege

3. FOLLY:

    (A) foolishness
    (B) grunt
    (C) regulation
    (D) verdict

4. SENTIMENT:

    (A) brink
    (B) feeling
    (C) ideal
    (D) scoop

Synonyms strategies checklist

Check below whether or not you used each strategy.

Did you...	Yes	No
1. Use positive or negative?	___	___
2. Think of where you have heard the word before?	___	___
3. Use roots or word parts?	___	___

Sentence Completions practice

1. After many hours of debate, the jury finally decided on the ------- of not guilty.

    (A) blunder
    (B) devotion
    (C) sensation
    (D) verdict

2. Before students leave on a fieldtrip, they must have the -------- of their parents.

    (A) ability
    (B) brink
    (C) consent
    (D) lure

3. Because many students didn't understand the topic, the teacher ---------.

    (A) decided to review it one more time
    (B) came to school late
    (C) wore a white shirt to school
    (D) packed a healthy snack

Sentence Completions strategies checklist

Check below whether or not you used each strategy.

Did you…	Yes	No
1. Underline a key word or phrase in EVERY question?	___	___
2. Look for sentences showing a change in direction (and circle the word that shows that contrast)?	___	___
3. Look for sentences showing sequence or cause?	___	___
4. Use our strategies for synonyms if you didn't know one or more of the answer choices?	___	___

Reading Comprehension practice

Reading passage practice

As you work through this passage, please remember to:

- Mark questions "S" or "G" before you read the passage
- Answer specific questions first and then general questions
- Use ruling out

Questions #1-5

1   The world changed forever in 1879 when Thomas Edison created the carbon
2 filament light bulb. There had been earlier attempts at producing light bulbs, but they
3 either burned for a very short period of time or were made of materials that were very
4 expensive. Mr. Edison's light bulb was the first to offer the hope of electric light to
5 ordinary Americans.
6   Thomas Edison's light bulb was a type of light bulb referred to as incandescent. In
7 incandescent bulbs electricity is sent through a wire that is called the filament. This
8 filament becomes very hot and creates a glow or light. The problem with incandescent
9 light bulbs is that they use a lot of electricity for the amount of light that they produce.
10 Incandescent light bulbs also give off a lot of heat which means that in the summertime
11 an air conditioner must work extra hard to cool a home that uses incandescent light
12 bulbs.
13   There are several types of light bulbs that are available that use less electricity and
14 produce less heat than an incandescent light bulb. Fluorescent light bulbs are one
15 example. In the past, fluorescent lights created a harsh light and a lot of noise. This is
16 no longer the case, though. Fluorescent light bulbs are more expensive than
17 incandescent light bulbs, but they last a lot longer and have lower energy costs. Another
18 option is LED bulbs. They can also create a warm light and save energy.
19   Even though there are now great alternatives, most houses in America still use
20 incandescent bulbs. If every house in America were to switch to more energy efficient
21 bulbs, though, just think of all the energy we could save. The best way to convince
22 people to switch light bulbs is to educate them about how great energy efficient bulbs
23 are these days.

1. Which statement best reflects the main idea of this passage?

   (A) It is important to convince people to switch to energy efficient light bulbs.
   (B) Incandescent light bulbs use a lot of energy.
   (C) Thomas Edison should never have invented the light bulb.
   (D) LED light bulbs are more energy efficient than incandescent light bulbs.

2. It can be inferred from the third paragraph (lines 13-18) that fluorescent light bulbs

   (A) use a lot of energy.
   (B) were invented by Thomas Edison.
   (C) have improved recently.
   (D) were the first type of light bulb.

3. In this passage, incandescent light bulbs can best be characterized as

   (A) cold.
   (B) important.
   (C) unused.
   (D) wasteful.

4. The author implies that convincing people to switch away from incandescent light bulbs will lead to

   (A) lower electrical rates.
   (B) less overall energy use.
   (C) lower prices for LED bulbs.
   (D) other kinds of bulbs being developed.

5. The function of the second paragraph (lines 6-12) is to

   (A) introduce a mystery.
   (B) explain why incandescent bulbs are not efficient.
   (C) summarize the main idea of the passage.
   (D) provide an argument against the author's main point.

Math practice

Quantitative Reasoning and Mathematics Achievement strategies

Our basic strategies for the math sections on the ISEE are:

- Estimate – this is a multiple-choice test!
- If there are variables in the answer choices, try plugging in your own numbers
- If they ask for the value of a variable, plug in answer choices

Quantitative Reasoning and Mathematics Achievement practice

1. Which expression correctly applies the distributive property to find the value of $12 \times (14 + 22)$?

    (A) $(12 \times 14) + (12 \times 22)$
    (B) $(12 \times 14) + 22$
    (C) $12 \times 14 + 22$
    (D) $22 + (12 \times 14)$

2. Otis had $4\frac{3}{8}$ cups of flour. He used $2\frac{1}{2}$ cups of this flour to make a cake. How many cups of flour did he have left?

    (A) $1\frac{7}{8}$

    (B) $2\frac{1}{8}$

    (C) $2\frac{1}{4}$

    (D) $2\frac{1}{2}$

3. If $6n + 6 = 24$, then what is the value of n?

    (A) 1
    (B) 2
    (C) 3
    (D) 4

4. Use the given number line.

Point B represents the average of point A and another number. What is that other number?

(A) 16
(B) 18
(C) 24
(D) 28

5. The figure below was created by adding four congruent triangles to a square.

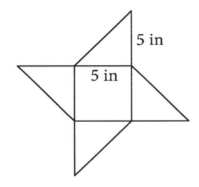

5 in

5 in

What is the area of the entire shape?

(A) 25 in²
(B) 75 in²
(C) 100 in²
(D) 125 in²

Workout #11 Answers

Vocabulary

Roots questions

1. *Emigrate* means "to move out of a country".

2. Other words with the *ques/quis/quir* root include *question, query, inquisition, inquiry, inquisitive*. You may have thought of some other words as well.

Words to remember questions

1. We give babies pacifiers in order to stop them from crying.

2. Answers will vary. A prim person finds it very important to be "proper" and always follow the rules.

Verbal Reasoning practice

Synonyms practice

1. C is the correct answer choice. The *reg* root means "to rule" and someone who is *regal* has the manner of someone who is used to ruling.

2. B is the correct answer choice. This is a word to remember from workout #10 so please review these words if you missed this question.

3. A is the correct answer choice. This is a word to remember from workout #4 so please review those words if you missed this question.

4. B is the correct answer choice. The word *sentiment* has the root *sent* which means "to feel". A sentiment is a feeling.

Sentence Completions practice

1. D is the correct answer choice. If you didn't know what the word *verdict* meant, you could have used ruling out. *Blunder, devotion,* and *sensation* do not relate to guilty or not guilty, so that leaves us only with *verdict*. The word *verdict* has the root *ver* which means "truth". A *verdict* is what a person (or group of people) believes to be true.

2. C is the correct answer choice. This would be another good question for using ruling out if you didn't know what *consent* means. *Consent* means "approval".

3. A is the correct answer choice. This sentence beings with the word "because" which tells us that it has a cause relationship. The beginning of the sentence talks about the students not understanding the topic, so what would that most directly lead to? The teacher reviewing the topic.

Reading Comprehension practice

Reading passage practice

1. A is the correct answer choice. For general questions, we look to the last sentence of the passage for the correct answer. Answer choice A is most closely related to the last sentence.

2. C is the correct answer choice. The passage states, "In the past, fluorescent lights created a harsh light and a lot of noise. This is no longer the case." This implies that fluorescent bulbs have improved.

3. D is the correct answer choice. The passage tells us that incandescent light bulbs use a lot of energy for the amount of light they produce and produce unwanted heat. This is best summed up by the word "wasteful".

4. B is the correct answer choice. The passage tells us, "If every house in America were to switch to more energy efficient bulbs, though, just think of all the energy we could save." Answer choices A, C, and D could very well happen, but they are not mentioned in the passage, so they are not the correct answer choices.

5. B is the correct answer choice. The second paragraph gives an explanation of why incandescent bulbs use a lot of energy for the amount of light that they produce.

Math practice

Quantitative Reasoning and Mathematics Achievement practice

1. A is the correct answer choice. Answer choices B-D not only do not show the distributive property correctly, they wouldn't even give the same value as the expression in the question.

2. A is the correct answer choice. In order to answer this question, we first have to get a common denominator for the fraction part of the mixed numbers. Since 2 and 8 both go into 8, that will be our common denominator. We can leave $4\frac{3}{8}$ as is, but we need to turn $2\frac{1}{2}$ into $2\frac{4}{8}$. The problem we run into now is that we cannot subtract $\frac{4}{8}$ from $\frac{3}{8}$. This means that we will have to borrow from the 4. Here is what the math looks like:

$$4\frac{3}{8} = 3 + 1 + \frac{3}{8} = 3 + \frac{8}{8} + \frac{3}{8} = 3\frac{11}{8}$$

Now we can complete the subtraction problem:

$$3\frac{11}{8} - 2\frac{4}{8} = 1\frac{7}{8}$$

3. C is the correct answer choice. Since we are asked for the value of a variable, we can plug in the answer choices and see which one makes the equation true. If we plug in 1 for n (answer choice A), we would get $6(1) + 6 = 24$. This is not true, so we can eliminate answer choice A. Now let's try plugging in 2 for n (answer choice B). This gives us $6(2) + 6 = 24$. This is also not a true statement so answer choice B can be ruled out. Now let's try choice C and plug in 3 for n. We get $6(3) + 6 = 24$. This is true so answer choice C is correct.

4. D is the correct answer choice. For this question, we first have to determine the scale of the number line from the points that are marked. Since there are 5 segments between 20 and 30 on the number line we know that the number line must count by twos. This means that Point A represents 20 and Point B represents 24. Now we have to use the fact that the average of two numbers is halfway in between the two numbers. This means that if Point A is 4 less than Point B, then the other point must be 4 greater than Point B. Since Point B represents 24, the other number must be 28.

5. B is the correct answer choice. In order to answer this question we need to find the area of the square and then add the area of the four triangles. Since each side of the square is 5 inches, the area of the square is $5 \times 5 = 25$ in². The area of each triangle is $\frac{1}{2} \times 5 \times 5$. If we do the math here, we wind up with a fraction. It is easier to multiply the whole thing by 4 since there are 4 triangles and use the associative property. The area of the four triangles is $4(\frac{1}{2} \times 5 \times 5) = (4 \times \frac{1}{2}) \times (5 \times 5) = 2 \times 25 = 50$ in². Now we add the area of the square (25 in²) and the area of the four triangles (50 in²) for a total area of 75 in².

Workout #12

Vocabulary

Roots

Below are some roots. I will give you the definition of the root and then two examples of words that have that root. I will give you the definition of each word and then you need to write in an example sentence or a memory trick you will use to remember the meaning of the word. At the end of the roots section, I will ask a question or two that gets you thinking about the roots and their meanings. Then we have the "Words to Remember!" section. These are three words that you need to memorize – I will give you the words and an example sentence, and then you need to answer a question or two about the words.

Be sure to make flashcards (or keep a list) of any words that you don't know. You will be responsible for knowing and applying the definitions of all the roots and words that you have learned as you move through the workouts.

Root: *chron*
Definition – time
Examples:
Chronic – happening or coming back frequently
Sentence or memory trick:

Synchronize – to happen at the same time
Sentence or memory trick:

Root: *don*
Definition – to give
Examples:
Donate – to give to a good cause without expecting something in return
Sentence or memory trick:

Donor – a person who donates
Sentence or memory trick:

Roots questions

1. If *synchronized* means "at the same time", then what do you think the *syn* root means?

2. What do you think a *chronometer* is?

Words to remember!

Exquisite – beautiful and rare
Example: I am jealous of her exquisite taste in clothing.

Drowsy – sleepy
Example: It is hard not to feel drowsy on a warm summer afternoon.

Hoist – to lift
Example: It is difficult to hoist a jug of water over your head.

Words to remember question

1. Would you want to go to bed early if you were *drowsy* or *exquisite*?

Verbal Reasoning practice

Now that you are more familiar with the strategies, we will skip right to the practice questions. You should try to apply strategy as you work through the practice questions. After you complete the practice, use the strategy checklists to make sure you are developing good habits.

Synonyms practice

1. EMIGRATE:

   (A) attract
   (B) disrupt
   (C) explain
   (D) move

2. ERUPT:

    (A) burst
    (B) decline
    (C) emphasize
    (D) report

3. INQUIRE:

    (A) ask
    (B) endorse
    (C) illuminate
    (D) prescience

4. ENDORSE:

    (A) contract
    (B) interrupt
    (C) question
    (D) support

Synonyms strategies checklist

Check below whether or not you used each strategy.

Did you…	Yes	No
1. Use positive or negative?	___	___
2. Think of where you have heard the word before?	___	___
3. Use roots or word parts?	___	___

Sentence Completions practice

1. It was unusual for Carol to disagree with another person or show any signs of --------.

   (A) cohesion
   (B) dissent
   (C) imagination
   (D) rehearsal

2. In hospitals it is important that instruments be cleaned -------- in order to prevent passing germs between patients.

   (A) concisely
   (B) primly
   (C) thoroughly
   (D) unconsciously

3. Although most animals eat with their heads in an upright position, flamingoes ---------.

   (A) consume a diet of mainly fish
   (B) are one of the more brightly colored animals
   (C) can only eat with their heads upside down
   (D) do not migrate far

Sentence Completions strategies checklist

Check below whether or not you used each strategy.

Did you...	Yes	No
1. Underline a key word or phrase in EVERY question?	___	___
2. Look for sentences showing a change in direction (and circle the word that shows that contrast)?	___	___
3. Look for sentences showing sequence or cause?	___	___
4. Use our strategies for synonyms if you didn't know one or more of the answer choices?	___	___

Reading Comprehension practice

Reading passage practice

As you work through this passage, please remember to:

- Mark questions "S" or "G" before you read the passage
- Answer specific questions first and then general questions
- Use ruling out

Questions #1-5

1   In 2011, Dr. Richard Freund proclaimed that his team of researchers had found
2 the lost city of Atlantis. It was located in the marshlands of Spain. He developed a
3 theory that a tsunami, or large wave from the ocean, had covered the city of Atlantis
4 several thousand years ago. This sounds like a very exciting discovery – until you start
5 to read the writings of other scientists who claim to have "discovered the lost city of
6 Atlantis".
7   A team of Japanese researchers say that they found granite rock deep in the ocean
8 off the coast of Brazil. Since granite normally only forms on land, the Japanese team
9 concluded that this land must have once been above water. They suggested this land
10 was the continent that Atlantis existed upon before it sunk into the sea. Another
11 researcher, Robert Sarmast, makes the case that the island of Cyprus was the site of the
12 city of Atlantis. Currently, Cyprus is an island formed from the top of a mountain that
13 just sticks out of the Mediterranean Sea. Robert Sarmast thinks that more of the
14 mountain was previously above water and Atlantis was located there.
15   Complicating matters is the fact that we can't be sure that Atlantis ever really
16 existed. Around 2,600 years ago, a Greek man named Solon travelled to Egypt and
17 translated historical records. In these records was the story of city lost to the sea. This
18 city was the beginning of all human societies. A couple hundred years later, Plato
19 included a story of a lost city in his writings. Were Solon and Plato sharing a legend
20 that was based on fact? Were they repeating a story that was simply made up? As long
21 as there is doubt, people will continue to be fascinated by the search for a lost city.

1. The main purpose of the passage is to

   (A) describe the city of Atlantis in detail.
   (B) determine the exact location of Atlantis.
   (C) discuss lost cities.
   (D) introduce an interesting mystery.

2. In line 17, the word "records" comes closest in meaning to

   (A) cities.
   (B) documents.
   (C) seas.
   (D) villas.

3. The passage implies that Dr. Richard Freund

   (A) claims that Atlantis existed off the coast of Brazil.
   (B) discovered the real Atlantis.
   (C) is just one of many scientists that claim to have discovered Atlantis.
   (D) leads a team of Japanese researchers.

4. Robert Sarmast clearly thinks that

   (A) land features change over time.
   (B) Atlantis is just a myth.
   (C) Plato said that Atlantis could be found on the island of Cyprus.
   (D) Atlantis will be found in an area with granite.

5. Why does the passage suggest that people are interested in the lost city of Atlantis?

   (A) People love a question without a definite answer.
   (B) There is buried treasure in the city of Atlantis.
   (C) Scientists keep people interested.
   (D) Many people read the writings of Plato.

Math practice

Quantitative Reasoning and Mathematics Achievement strategies

Our basic strategies for the math sections on the ISEE are:

- Estimate – this is a multiple-choice test!
- If there are variables in the answer choices, try plugging in your own numbers
- If they ask for the value of a variable, plug in answer choices

Quantitative Reasoning and Mathematics Achievement practice

1. There are a total of 32 marbles in a bag. They are green, yellow, or white. If there are 9 green marbles and 12 yellow marbles, then how many white marbles must there be in the bag?

   (A) 7
   (B) 9
   (C) 10
   (D) 11

2. Which fraction is smallest?

   (A) $\dfrac{6}{9}$

   (B) $\dfrac{3}{5}$

   (C) $\dfrac{4}{9}$

   (D) $\dfrac{7}{11}$

3. Use the input/output table below in order to answer the question.

Input (x)	Output (y)
3	7
6	10
11	15
20	24
25	29

What rule determines each output?

(A) $(2 \times x) + 1 = y$
(B) $(3 \times x) - 2 = y$
(C) $x + 4 = y$
(D) $x + 5 = y$

4. Use the graph below.

Books in Library by Genre

= 4,000 books

How many more science fiction books than poetry books does the library have?

(A) 8,000
(B) 12,000
(C) 16,000
(D) 24,000

5. A machine can stamp 4 envelopes in one second. How many envelopes can the machine stamp in one minute?

(A) 60
(B) 120
(C) 180
(D) 240

Workout #12 Answers

Vocabulary

Roots questions

1. The *syn* root means "same".

2. A *chronometer* is something that measures time, such as a watch.

Words to remember question

1. You would want to go to bed early if you were *drowsy*.

Verbal Reasoning practice

Synonyms practice

1. D is the correct answer choice. The root *migr* means "to move". *Emigrate* means more specifically to move out of a place, but on the ISEE all of the synonyms are only one word.

2. A is the correct answer choice. The word *erupt* has two roots – *e* means "out of" and *rupt* means "break" – so *erupt* literally means to break out of and *burst* comes closest to this meaning.

3. A is the correct answer choice. The word *inquire* has the *quir* root that means "to ask".

4. D is the correct answer choice. This is a word to remember from workout #7 so please review those words if you missed this question.

Sentence Completions practice

1. B is the correct answer choice. We are looking for a word that goes along with *disagree*. The word *dissent* shares the same root so it is a good bet. The word *dissent* has two roots – *dis* which is negative and *sent* which means "feelings" – so it means to have feelings against something.

2. C is the correct answer choice. It is important that instruments be cleaned completely, or thoroughly. If you did not know the meaning of the word *thorough*, it was a word to remember from workout #9 so please review those words.

3. C is the correct answer choice. The word *although* tells us that this is a sentence showing contrast. The beginning of the sentence tells us about animals that eat with their heads upright, so we are looking for the answer choice that says the opposite of this.

Reading Comprehension practice

Reading passage practice

1. D is the correct answer choice. Answer choices A and B are not possible – the passage tells us that no one even knows for sure if Atlantis really existed. Answer choice C is too broad. The passage is not discussing lost cities in general but rather focuses on Atlantis. We are left with choice D.

2. B is the correct answer choice. Since this is a vocabulary in context question, we will go back and cross out the word "records" in the passage and then plug in answer choices. It would only make sense to translate *documents* so that is the correct answer choice.

3. C is the correct answer choice. Answer choices A and D are traps – the passage discusses them but not in reference to Dr. Freund. We can eliminate them. So now we have to decide whether the author believes that Dr. Freund really discovered Atlantis or whether he is just one of many claiming to have discovered Atlantis. Since the author doesn't even say that Atlantis is real, we can rule out choice B. We are left with choice C.

4. A is the correct answer choice. If we go back to where the passage discusses Robert Sarmast, it says that Cyprus is now just the tip of a mountain above water but that Robert Sarmast thinks that more of the mountaintop was exposed before. This implies that he believes that land features can change over time.

5. A is the correct answer choice. The passage states that, "As long as there is doubt, people will continue to be fascinated by the search for a lost city." Answer choice A best restates this idea.

Math practice

Quantitative Reasoning and Mathematics Achievement practice

1. D is the correct answer choice. In this question, we have a total and the number of items in a couple of groups. In order to find the number of items in the missing group, we need to use subtraction. If we subtract the known groups from the total we get $32 - 9 - 12 = 11$. There must be 11 white marbles in the bag.

2. C is the correct answer choice. The trick to this question is that it would be very hard to find a common denominator. However, we can easily figure out whether each fraction is greater than or less than one-half. Since $\frac{6}{12}$ is equal to one-half, we know that $\frac{6}{9}$ has to be greater than one-half (a smaller denominator makes a fraction larger if the numerator remains the same). Now let's look at answer choice B. The fraction $\frac{3}{6}$ is equal to one-half so $\frac{3}{5}$ is greater than one-half. Now let's move onto choice C. The fraction $\frac{4}{8}$ is equal to one-half, so $\frac{4}{9}$ is less than one-half. Now we look at choice D. Since $\frac{7}{14}$ is equal to one-half, $\frac{7}{11}$ is greater than one-half. Only answer choice C is less than one-half, so it is the smallest fraction.

3. C is the correct answer choice. The trick to this question is that three of the rules (answer choices A, B, and C) work for the first input/output pair. If you try the second input/output pair, however, you will find that only the rule given in choice C works. Since the rule must apply to ALL input/output pairs answer choice C is correct.

4. A is the correct answer choice. The important part of answering this question is to use the given key. At the bottom of the pictograph, we can see that one book picture is equal to 4,000 actual books. Since there are two more book pictures for science fiction than for poetry, we need to multiply $4,000 \times 2 = 8,000$.

5. D is the correct answer. In order to answer this question we have to convert from envelopes per second to envelopes per minute. Since there are 60 seconds in a minute, we multiply 4×60 and get that the machine stamps 240 envelopes per minute.

Workout #13

Vocabulary

Roots

Below are some roots. I will give you the definition of the root and then two examples of words that have that root. I will give you the definition of each word and then you need to write in an example sentence or a memory trick you will use to remember the meaning of the word. At the end of the roots section, I will ask a question or two that gets you thinking about the roots and their meanings. Then we have the "Words to Remember!" section. These are three words that you need to memorize – I will give you the words and an example sentence, and then you need to answer a question or two about the words.

Be sure to make flashcards (or keep a list) of any words that you don't know. You will be responsible for knowing and applying the definitions of all the roots and words that you have learned as you move through the workouts.

Root: *dic*
Definition – to speak
Examples:
Dictate – to speak words that are to be written down
Sentence or memory trick:

Contradict – to speak against something or say that someone is wrong
Sentence or memory trick:

Root: *dem*
Definition – people
Examples:
Democracy – rule by the people
Sentence or memory trick:

Epidemic – a disease that has spread throughout a population
Sentence or memory trick:

Roots question

1. If the root *dem* means "people" and *democracy* means "rule by the people", what do you think the *cracy* root means?

2. If *contradict* means "to speak against someone" or "say something is not true", what do you think the *contra* root means?

Words to remember!

Hurl – to throw
Example: The pitcher hurled the ball toward home plate.

Ignorant – without knowledge
Example: Thelma drove the wrong way down the road because she was ignorant of the fact that it was a one-way road.

Cultivate – to encourage growth
Example: Plants are best cultivated where there is plenty of sunshine and water.

Words to remember questions

1. Should you *cultivate* or *hurl* a relationship with your friends?

2. Can you think of a word that means the opposite of *ignorant*?

Verbal Reasoning practice

Now that you are more familiar with the strategies, we will skip right to the practice questions. You should try to apply strategy as you work through the practice questions. After you complete the practice, use the strategy checklists to make sure you are developing good habits.

Synonyms practice

1. CHRONIC:

    (A) drowsy
    (B) frequent
    (C) pacified
    (D) secure

2. DROWSY:

    (A) devoted
    (B) homely
    (C) sleepy
    (D) tense

3. FOSTER:

    (A) encourage
    (B) inquire
    (C) meddle
    (D) replace

4. PRIM:

    (A) favorable
    (B) ideal
    (C) objective
    (D) proper

Synonyms strategies checklist

Check below whether or not you used each strategy.

Did you…	Yes	No
1. Use positive or negative?	___	___
2. Think of where you have heard the word before?	___	___
3. Use roots or word parts?	___	___

Sentence Completions practice

1. A space shuttle launch is a very delicate operation and can only happen when there are --------- weather conditions.

    (A) barren
    (B) favorable
    (C) frigid
    (D) rugged

2. Home magazines often describe homes that are -------- with features such as large windows, plenty of space, and no clutter.

    (A) chronic
    (B) gentle
    (C) humane
    (D) ideal

3. Although artist Mary Cassatt was born in America, ---------.

    (A) many of paintings featured women and children
    (B) her father was a stockbroker
    (C) she spent most of her adult life living in France
    (D) she studied many master painters

Sentence Completions strategies checklist

Check below whether or not you used each strategy.

Did you...	Yes	No
1. Underline a key word or phrase in EVERY question?	___	___
2. Look for sentences showing a change in direction (and circle the word that shows that contrast)?	___	___
3. Look for sentences showing sequence or cause?	___	___
4. Use our strategies for synonyms if you didn't know one or more of the answer choices?	___	___

Reading Comprehension practice

Reading passage practice

As you work through the passage on the next page, please remember to:

- Mark questions "S" or "G" before you read the passage
- Answer specific questions first and then general questions
- Use ruling out

1   When I was eight years old, my parents decided that it was time for me to start
2 going to sleepaway camp. There was no question of which camp I would attend. Both
3 my father and grandfather had attended Towering Pines Camp for Boys in the woods
4 of Northern Minnesota. I had heard tales of ghost stories around the fire with s'mores,
5 early morning raids of the girls' camp across the lake, and canoe wars where the last
6 canoe still floating held the victors.

7   What no one told me about was the swim test on the first day of camp. On the first
8 morning, I awoke to the shrill whistle of our counselor Davy. He was a college student
9 who seemed about ten feet tall and strong enough to crush three of us boys at one time.

10   "Up and at them, men! Get your bathing suits on, we are going to find out who
11 can swim and who is going to sink." This did not sound good. I had been taking swim
12 lessons for years, but not with all that much success. I was new to camp and didn't know
13 anybody. I didn't want to be the kid who failed the swim test for the next six weeks.

14   We went down to the waterfront and a cold wind whipped off the lake. I stuck my
15 toe in the water. The water was so cold that it sent shivers up my spine. I thought of all
16 the reasons I could use to get out of this swim test. Maybe I could fake a cold and get
17 sent to the infirmary? Perhaps I could pretend to sprain my ankle?

18   I didn't have much time to think about it, though. While I was coming up with
19 excuses, Davy had silently walked up behind me. Suddenly I felt a large hand on my
20 back. Before I could even react, that hand shoved me into the ice cold water. I came up
21 in shock. But then something magical happened. My arms went from waving in the air
22 to stroking through the water like they never had before. I watched the boys in front of
23 me get closer and closer. One by one, I passed them. Soon I was the first person pulling
24 myself out of the water on the other side. Davy placed a crown on my head made out
25 of pine branches and raised one of my tired arms in triumph.

1. The main purpose of this passage was to

    (A) describe the swimming test at one camp.
    (B) share the experience of one camper.
    (C) relate the climate of Northern Minnesota.
    (D) discuss strategies for passing the swim test.

2. As described in the passage, Davy can best be characterized as

    (A) kind.
    (B) quiet.
    (C) threatening.
    (D) wary.

3. In line 8, the word "shrill" is closest in meaning to

    (A) bent.
    (B) cordial.
    (C) loud.
    (D) tidy.

4. In this passage, the author's attitude

    (A) remains unchanged.
    (B) is frightened throughout the passage.
    (C) can be described as bold in the beginning and uncaring at the end.
    (D) changes from scared to proud.

5. The purpose of the last sentence (lines 24-25) is to

    (A) provide an exciting ending.
    (B) summarize the main points of the passage.
    (C) provide evidence for an argument.
    (D) leave the reader with questions.

Math practice

Quantitative Reasoning and Mathematics Achievement strategies

Our basic strategies for the math sections on the ISEE are:

- Estimate – this is a multiple-choice test!
- If there are variables in the answer choices, try plugging in your own numbers
- If they ask for the value of a variable, plug in answer choices

Quantitative Reasoning and Mathematics Achievement practice

1. Felicia has to make a store display with cans. If there are to be 24 rows each with 36 cans, which expression would allow Felicia to figure out how many cans she will need to create the display?

    (A) $36 \div 24$
    (B) 36×24
    (C) $36 + 24$
    (D) $36 - 24$

2. Which fraction has the same value as 0.06?

    (A) $\dfrac{1}{600}$

    (B) $\dfrac{6}{100}$

    (C) $\dfrac{1}{6}$

    (D) $\dfrac{6}{10}$

3. What value for ■ would make the equation $3 \times (■ + 5) = 18$ true?

    (A) 1
    (B) 2
    (C) 3
    (D) 6

4. Claude's class went on a trip to an art museum and were asked to collect data about what they saw. Claude's teacher asked them to list their data in categories.

CLAUDE'S OBSERVATIONS

kinds of paint used: watercolors, oil, charcoal, acrylic

types of paintings: portrait, still life, abstract

?

Which type of information could be added to this observation list?

(A) number of visitors each day
(B) number of paintings in the museum
(C) dimensions of each painting
(D) time periods in which paintings were created

5. Ana drew a rectangle with an area of 14 cm^2. Which could be the dimensions of this rectangle?

(A) 8 cm × 6 cm
(B) 9 cm × 5 cm
(C) 7 cm × 2 cm
(D) 4 cm × 10 cm

Workout #13 Answers

Vocabulary

Roots questions

1. The root *cracy* means "to rule". *Autocracy* is rule by one person and *theocracy* is rule by religious leaders.

2. The *contra* root means "against". A *controversy* is caused when people speak against one another.

Words to remember questions

1. You should *cultivate* your relationship with your friends. *Cultivate* can mean encouraging plants to grow as well as encouraging things that grow that are not physical objects.

2. Answers will vary, but a word like *educated* would be the opposite of *ignorant*.

Verbal Reasoning practice

Synonyms practice

1. B is the correct answer choice. The root *chron* means "time" so we know we are looking for a word that relates to time. Only answer choice B is related to time.

2. C is the correct answer choice. *Drowsy* is a word to remember from workout #12 so please review those words if you missed this question.

3. A is the correct answer choice. *Foster* is a word to remember from workout #11 so please review those words if you missed this question.

4. D is the correct answer choice. You may have been able to use context – have you ever heard someone described as prim and proper? Prim is also a word to remember from workout #11 so please review those words if you missed this question.

Sentence Completions practice

1. B is the correct answer choice. Perhaps the easiest strategy here is to fill in our own word. The beginning of the sentence tells us that a *launch* is delicate, so we might fill in that we need "good" weather conditions. The word *favorable* comes closest to the word good.

2. D is the correct answer choice. This sentence has a blank and then gives examples of the word that fits in the blank. What kind of homes would have large windows, plenty of space, and no clutter? *Ideal* ones.

3. C is the correct answer choice. We have the word *although* so we know that the end of the sentence has to contrast with the beginning of the sentence. The beginning of the sentence talks about her being born in America and answer choice C provides the contrast that she mainly lived in France as an adult.

Reading Comprehension practice

Reading passage practice

1. B is the correct answer choice. This is a narrative passage and the purpose is to share a story, or experience.

2. C is the correct answer choice. The passage tells us that Davy seems ten feet tall, capable of crushing boys, and that he pushes unsuspecting children into the water. *Threatening* best captures his character.

3. C is the correct answer choice. This is a vocabulary in context question so we go back to the passage and cross out the word "shrill" and fill in the answer choices. The sound of a whistle that can wake someone up would best be described as *loud*.

4. D is the correct answer choice. At the beginning of the passage, the author is scared of Davy and the cold water and what the other campers will think. At the end of the passage, he has come in first in the swimming test.

5. A is the correct answer choice. This is a passage that tells a story so we can rule out choices B and C because they are more appropriate for nonfiction writing. Then we have to decide whether the reader gets an exciting ending or is left with questions. The narrator ends with his triumph over the swimming test, so answer choice A is correct.

Math practice

Quantitative Reasoning and Mathematics Achievement practice

1. B is the correct answer choice. We are given the number of groups and the size of each group, so we should use multiplication to find the total.

2. B is the correct answer choice. The decimal represents six hundredths, which is equal to $\frac{6}{100}$. Since they are really just testing place value, the answer choices do not require you to reduce the fraction.

3. A is the correct answer choice. Since they are asking us for the value of a variable, we can plug in answer choices and see what works. Let's start with choice A. If we plug in 1 for ■ then we get $3 \times (1 + 5) = 18$ or $3 \times 6 = 18$. Since this is true, answer choice A is correct.

4. D is the correct answer choice. In this question, we are looking for qualitative data (data that is organized in categories) and not quantitative data (data that records numbers). Only answer choice D gives another category.

5. C is the correct answer choice. In order to find the area of a rectangle, we multiply the length times the width. Only choice C has two dimensions that would give us 14 when multiplied together.

Workout #14

Vocabulary

Roots

Below are some roots. I will give you the definition of the root and then two examples of words that have that root. I will give you the definition of each word and then you need to write in an example sentence or a memory trick you will use to remember the meaning of the word. At the end of the roots section, I will ask a question or two that gets you thinking about the roots and their meanings. Then we have the "Words to Remember!" section. These are three words that you need to memorize – I will give you the words and an example sentence, and then you need to answer a question or two about the words.

Be sure to make flashcards (or keep a list) of any words that you don't know. You will be responsible for knowing and applying the definitions of all the roots and words that you have learned as you move through the workouts.

Root: *fac/fic*
Definition – to make
Examples:
Fiction – a story that is made up (not true)
Sentence or memory trick:

Manufacture – to make
Sentence or memory trick:

Root: *form*
Definition – shape
Examples:
Transform – to change shape
Sentence or memory trick:

Reform – to reshape in a way that is better
Sentence or memory trick:

Roots questions

1. If the *man* root means "hand", what does the word *manufacture* literally mean?

2. What do you think it means to "formulate a plan"?

Words to remember!

Haven – a safe place
Example: In a storm, sea captains look out for a sheltered haven where their ships will be protected.

Envelop – to surround
Example: The fragile package was enveloped in thick wrapping paper so that it would not be damaged.

Jovial – joyous
Example: Santa Claus is known for being jovial with a hearty laugh and constant smile.

Words to remember questions

1. How do you think the word *envelope* relates to the word *envelop*?

2. Who is the most *jovial* person you know?

Verbal Reasoning practice

Now that you are more familiar with the strategies, we will skip right to the practice questions. You should try to apply strategy as you work through the practice questions. After you complete the practice, use the strategy checklists to make sure you are developing good habits.

Synonyms practice

1. CONTRADICT:

   (A) disagree
   (B) growl
   (C) regulate
   (D) synchronize

2. INQUISITIVE:

   (A) curious
   (B) elaborate
   (C) logical
   (D) meddlesome

3. IGNORANT:

   (A) drowsy
   (B) mournful
   (C) sensitive
   (D) uneducated

4. MANUFACTURE:

   (A) drench
   (B) make
   (C) ponder
   (D) regret

Synonyms strategies checklist

Check below whether or not you used each strategy.

Did you…	Yes	No
1. Use positive or negative?	___	___
2. Think of where you have heard the word before?	___	___
3. Use roots or word parts?	___	___

Sentence Completions practice

1. The United States government is a --------- in which the people elect the leaders.

    (A) baron
    (B) democracy
    (C) regime
    (D) tyrant

2. The beautifully sewn dress could best be described as --------.

    (A) bloated
    (B) contrary
    (C) exquisite
    (D) homely

3. The loud crash from upstairs led Sally to --------.

    (A) get ready for school
    (B) take her dog for a walk
    (C) choose a different breakfast cereal
    (D) go upstairs in order to see what could have fallen

Sentence Completions strategies checklist

Check below whether or not you used each strategy.

Did you...	Yes	No
1. Underline a key word or phrase in EVERY question?	___	___
2. Look for sentences showing a change in direction (and circle the word that shows that contrast)?	___	___
3. Look for sentences showing sequence or cause?	___	___
4. Use our strategies for synonyms if you didn't know one or more of the answer choices?	___	___

Reading Comprehension practice

Reading passage practice

As you work through the passage on the next page, please remember to:

- Mark questions "S" or "G" before you read the passage
- Answer specific questions first and then general questions
- Use ruling out

Questions #1-5

1   If you were a student learning about the planets in our solar system before 2006,
2 you probably would have learned that there were nine planets. You would have learned
3 that the ninth planet, and the farthest from the sun, was Pluto.

4   Pluto was first discovered in 1930. After the planet was discovered, it needed to be
5 named. An eleven-year-old girl, Venetia Burney, suggested that the planet be named
6 Pluto after the Roman god of the underworld. This name was accepted and so Pluto
7 came to be the only planet named by a child.

8   In 1977 doubts arose that Pluto was really a planet. Pluto is only about one-third
9 the size of Earth's moon. It is mainly made up of rock and ice. Starting in 1977,
10 scientists started discovering other objects in space that had similar properties. If they
11 wanted to call Pluto a planet then all of these other objects would also need to be called
12 planets.

13   In 1990, the Hubble Space Telescope began to travel through our solar system. It
14 has been recording new data about our solar system and sending it back to scientists to
15 study ever since. From the evidence collected by the Hubble Space Telescope, we now
16 know that there are several other small bodies made of rock and ice in our solar system.
17 In 2006, the International Astronomical Union decided that Pluto should no longer be
18 considered a planet. Rather, they created a new category of dwarf planets, or plutoids,
19 that Pluto would belong to.

20   Students today no longer learn that there are nine planets. There are now only
21 eight planets to be learned. Also, Neptune is now considered the farthest planet from
22 the sun in our solar system – Pluto no longer holds that honor.

1. Which answer choice best captures the main idea of this passage?

    (A) The Hubble Space Telescope has changed our thoughts on many planets.
    (B) Pluto was the only planet named by a child.
    (C) The International Astronomical Union should not have put Pluto in a different category.
    (D) Pluto is no longer considered the ninth planet in our solar system.

2. Which word best describes Pluto?

    (A) close.
    (B) green.
    (C) hot.
    (D) small.

3. The author states that Pluto can no longer be considered a planet because

    (A) there are too many other bodies that are similar to Pluto.
    (B) the definition of a planet was changed.
    (C) Pluto has many moons.
    (D) Venetia Burney suggested that Pluto wasn't really a planet.

4. In the fourth paragraph (lines 13-19) it is implied that before the Hubble Space Telescope was in use scientists did not know

    (A) that Pluto existed.
    (B) that other objects existed in space that were like Pluto.
    (C) just how far a space telescope could travel.
    (D) the importance of Pluto in our solar system.

5. It can be inferred from the passage that Neptune is

    (A) a small planet.
    (B) made of rock and ice.
    (C) the eighth farthest planet from the sun.
    (D) the ninth farthest planet from the sun.

Math practice

Quantitative Reasoning and Mathematics Achievement strategies

Our basic strategies for the math sections on the ISEE are:

- Estimate – this is a multiple-choice test!
- If there are variables in the answer choices, try plugging in your own numbers
- If they ask for the value of a variable, plug in answer choices

Quantitative Reasoning and Mathematics Achievement practice

1. What is the expression $3,000 - 285$ equal to?

    (A) 2715
    (B) 2725
    (C) 2735
    (D) 2745

2. Use the given number line.

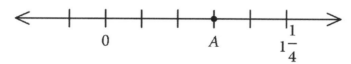

    What number does point A represent?

    (A) $\dfrac{1}{2}$

    (B) $\dfrac{3}{4}$

    (C) 1

    (D) $1\dfrac{1}{2}$

3. Lewis and Cory were riding their bikes at the same speed. If it took Lewis 20 minutes to ride 5 miles then how long would it take Cory to ride 6 miles?

(A) 16 minutes
(B) 18 minutes
(C) 22 minutes
(D) 24 minutes

4. Five classmates counted the number of marbles in their collections at home.

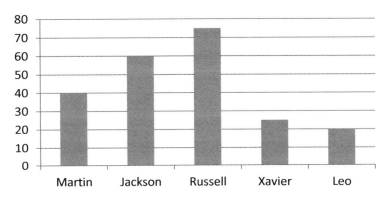

Based on the graph above, which of the following statements is true?

(A) The mean number of marbles is between 50 and 55
(B) The median is greater than the number of marbles in Jackson's collection
(C) The range is equal to the number of marbles in Martin's collection
(D) Jackson has as many marbles in his collection as Leo and Martin combined

5. Use the coordinate grid below to answer the question.

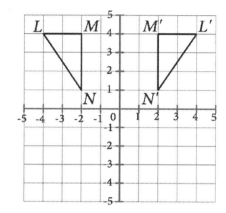

Which transformation(s) took place to create *L'M'N'* from *LMN*?

(A) a slide only
(B) a flip only
(C) a slide and then another slide
(D) a flip and then another flip

Workout #14 Answers

Vocabulary

Roots questions

1. The word *manufacture* literally means "to make by hand".

2. To *formulate* a plan means to come up with a plan.

Words to remember questions

1. An envelope *envelops* a letter or completely surrounds what is in it.

2. Answers will vary – someone who laughs a lot and loves joking around would be *jovial*.

Verbal Reasoning practice

Synonyms practice

1. A is the correct answer choice. The word *contradict* has two roots – *contra* means "against" and *dict* means "to speak" – so *contradict* literally means "to speak against", or disagree.

2. A is the correct answer choice. *Inquisitive* has the *quis* root in it which means "to ask". *Inquisitive* therefore describes someone who likes to ask questions, or is curious.

3. D is the correct answer choice. *Ignorant* is a word to remember from workout #13 so please review those words if you missed this question.

4. B is the correct answer choice. The word *manufacture* has the *fac* root in it which means "to make".

Sentence Completions practice

1. B is the correct answer. The word *democracy* has the root *dem* which means "people". You may have been tempted by *regime* because the *reg* root means "to rule", but in a regime the leader is most definitely NOT elected by the people.

2. C is the correct answer choice. If we use process of elimination, the words *bloated*, *contrary*, or *homely* would definitely not describe a dress that is beautifully sewn. *Exquisite* is a word to remember from workout #12 so please review these words if you didn't remember the meaning of exquisite.

3. D is the correct answer choice. This sentence has a cause relationship. The beginning of the sentence talks about a loud crash upstairs so we need to choose the action that would be most directly caused by a loud crash. Answer choice D comes closest.

Reading Comprehension practice

Reading passage practice

1. D is the correct answer choice. Answer choices A, B, and C contain details from the passage but not the main idea. If we look to the last sentence for our answer we can clearly see that answer choice D captures the main idea.

2. D is the correct answer choice. The passage tells us that "Pluto is only about one-third the size of Earth's moon". We can also use ruling out. Pluto was the planet farthest from the sun so we can rule out that it is close. The passage also tells us that it is rocky and icy, so we can rule out green and hot. We are left with choice D.

3. A is the correct answer choice. The passage tells us that "If they wanted to call Pluto a planet then all of these other objects would also need to be called planets". This provides evidence about why Pluto was put in a different category. Answer choice B is tempting but there is no evidence in the passage that the definition was changed.

4. B is the correct answer choice. The fourth paragraph tells us, "From the evidence collected by the Hubble Space Telescope, we now know that there are several other small bodies made of rock and ice in our solar system." This implies that before the Hubble Space Telescope we did not know about these small bodies that were like Pluto.

5. C is the correct answer choice. The passage tells us that Pluto was previously the ninth farthest planet from the sun and that now there are only eight planets and Neptune is the farthest from the sun. This implies that Neptune is the eighth farthest planet from the sun.

Math practice

Quantitative Reasoning and Mathematics Achievement practice

1. A is the correct answer choice. If you missed this question, go back and check to make sure that you borrowed correctly.

2. B is the correct answer choice. Since this is a number line problem, we need to use the points given to determine the scale. There are five segments between 0 and $1\frac{1}{4}$ so the number line must be counting by $\frac{1}{4}$. If we count up from 0, we would get that the first dash mark is equal to $\frac{1}{4}$, the second dash represents $\frac{1}{2}$, and the third dash (or point A) represents $\frac{3}{4}$.

3. D is the correct answer choice. We can use a proportion to solve since they were travelling at the same speed:

$$\frac{5 \text{ miles}}{20 \text{ minutes}} = \frac{6 \text{ miles}}{m \text{ minutes}}$$

Now we can cross-multiply and solve:

$$5 \times m = 20 \times 6$$
$$5m = 120$$
$$m = 24 \text{ minutes}$$

4. D is the correct answer choice. If you calculate the mean, it is 44, which allows us to eliminate choice A. The median is 40 marbles, which is not greater than the marbles in Jackson's collection, so choice B is out. The range is 55 and Martin has 40 marbles, so we can rule out choice C. Leo and Martin have 60 marbles combined and Jackson has 60 marbles, so choice D is correct.

5. B is the correct answer choice. To get from LMN to $L'M'N'$, we simply flip LMN across the y-axis.

Workout #15

Vocabulary

Roots

Below are some roots. I will give you the definition of the root and then two examples of words that have that root. I will give you the definition of each word and then you need to write in an example sentence or a memory trick you will use to remember the meaning of the word. At the end of the roots section, I will ask a question or two that gets you thinking about the roots and their meanings. Then we have the "Words to Remember!" section. These are three words that you need to memorize – I will give you the words and an example sentence, and then you need to answer a question or two about the words.

Be sure to make flashcards (or keep a list) of any words that you don't know. You will be responsible for knowing and applying the definitions of all the roots and words that you have learned as you move through the workouts.

Root: *uni*
Definition – one
Examples:
Uniform – all the same
Sentence or memory trick:

Unique – one of a kind
Sentence or memory trick:

Root: *claim/clam*
Definition – to shout
Examples:
Proclaim – to loudly declare
Sentence or memory trick:

Clamor – a loud noise
Sentence or memory trick:

Roots questions

1. How does the word *uniform* relate to the roots *uni* and *form*?

2. If *claim* means "to shout", what do you think *exclaim* means?

Words to remember!

Obstruct – to get in the way of
Example: A tree branch fell across the road and obstructed cars trying to drive down that street.

Morsel – a small piece of something
Example: Chocolate is so good that sometimes you only need a small morsel.

Pact – an agreement between two parties
Example: Sarah and Daniel made a pact that they would both remember to do their homework every night for one week.

Words to remember questions

1. Do you think a *morsel* of bread would be satisfying?

2. What do you think it means to *obstruct justice*?

Verbal Reasoning practice

Now that you are more familiar with the strategies, we will skip right to the practice questions. You should try to apply strategy as you work through the practice questions. After you complete the practice, use the strategy checklists to make sure you are developing good habits.

Synonyms practice

1. HURL:

   (A) envelop
   (B) inspect
   (C) reform
   (D) throw

2. FORMLESS:

   (A) inclined
   (B) shapeless
   (C) unconnected
   (D) unessential

3. CLAMOR:

   (A) donor
   (B) fiction
   (C) prologue
   (D) noise

4. HOIST:

   (A) attract
   (B) lift
   (C) migrate
   (D) request

Synonyms strategies checklist

Check below whether or not you used each strategy.

Did you...	Yes	No
1. Use positive or negative?	___	___
2. Think of where you have heard the word before?	___	___
3. Use roots or word parts?	___	___

Sentence Completions practice

1. If even a tiny bit of food is left on the floor that ------- could attract mice and other critters.

    (A) brink
    (B) calamity
    (C) morsel
    (D) verdict

2. The Boston harbor is surrounded by land on three sides which makes it a safe ------- for boats during storms.

    (A) haven
    (B) merger
    (C) pantomime
    (D) rupture

3. Although Marilyn Monroe was often dismissed as a serious actress, she ---------.

    (A) was born Norma Jean
    (B) lived during the 1960s
    (C) actually displayed great talent
    (D) is famous for her blonde hair

Sentence Completions strategies checklist

Check below whether or not you used each strategy.

Did you...	Yes	No
1. Underline a key word or phrase in EVERY question?	___	___
2. Look for sentences showing a change in direction (and circle the word that shows that contrast)?	___	___
3. Look for sentences showing sequence or cause?	___	___
4. Use our strategies for synonyms if you didn't know one or more of the answer choices?	___	___

Reading Comprehension practice

Reading passage practice

Now we will move onto answering questions about passages. As you work through this passage, please remember to:

- Mark questions "S" or "G" before you read the passage
- Answer specific questions first and then general questions
- Use ruling out

Questions #1-5

1   In 1892, Mitchell, South Dakota was a city with only 3,000 citizens. It had been a
2 city for only twelve years. Its inhabitants wanted a way to spread the word that South
3 Dakota had a great climate for running an agricultural business, such as farming. They
4 decided that they would build a palace from corn stalks in order to do this.
5   The palace was designed to be a place where local residents could gather for a fall
6 festival. There would be live entertainment to celebrate the end of the crop-growing
7 season. It would provide a place for the residents of rural Mitchell to come together.
8   The popularity of the Corn Palace grew. In 1905 a larger one had to built, but the
9 crowds kept growing. Yet another larger corn palace was completed in 1921. It was
10 completed just in time for Mitchell to host the boys state basketball tournament. At that
11 time, the Corn Palace was considered to have the best basketball arena in the upper
12 Midwest region of the United States. The Corn Palace built in 1921 still stands today.
13 In the 1930s additional artistic features were added in order to recreate the drama of the
14 original corn palace.
15   Today the Corn Palace hosts many events, such as basketball tournaments and live
16 performances. It is also decorated each year with various colored corns in order to make
17 it "the agricultural show-place of the world". Murals are created from corn grains in
18 thirteen different colors. At the end of August every year, the old murals are stripped
19 from the walls of the Corn Palace. By October, a new mural has emerged in the same
20 space. Each year the mural has a different theme, such as "America's Destinations".
21   About 500,000 people come every year to see these murals and visit the Corn
22 Palace. If the early creators of the Corn Palace wanted to create a gathering place and
23 spread the word about South Dakota, they have certainly succeeded.

1. This passage is mainly concerned with

    (A) introducing an argument.
    (B) providing conflicting viewpoints.
    (C) convincing the reader to take an action.
    (D) describing an interesting place.

2. According to the passage, what was one reason for building the Corn Palace?

    (A) Farmers had grown too much corn.
    (B) Local citizens wanted to others to know about farming in South Dakota.
    (C) The town needed a place to host basketball tournaments.
    (D) Corn is a strong building material.

3. In line 2, the word "inhabitants" is closest in meaning to

    (A) neighbors.
    (B) observers.
    (C) residents.
    (D) speakers.

4. Which of the following questions can be answered with information in the passage?

    (A) How many people visit the Corn Palace each year?
    (B) Where do most visitors come from?
    (C) Who won the first basketball game in the Corn Palace?
    (D) How many people built the original Corn Palace?

5. The Corn Palace as described in the passage is

    (A) no longer in use.
    (B) frequently changing.
    (C) very small.
    (D) completely rebuilt every year.

Math practice

Quantitative Reasoning and Mathematics Achievement strategies

Our basic strategies for the math sections on the ISEE are:

- Estimate – this is a multiple-choice test!
- If there are variables in the answer choices, try plugging in your own numbers
- If they ask for the value of a variable, plug in answer choices

Quantitative Reasoning and Mathematics Achievement practice

1. Which expression is equal to $3 \times (4 + 6)$?

   (A) $12 + 6$
   (B) $18 + 4$
   (C) 3×10
   (D) 4×9

2. What is the value of $4.3 - 3.6$?

   (A) 0.7
   (B) 1.0
   (C) 1.3
   (D) 1.6

3. Which story would best fit the equation $24 \div 3 = 8$?

   (A) There are 24 rows each with 8 cans. How many total cans are there?
   (B) There are 24 cans arranged in 3 equal rows. How many cans are in each row?
   (C) I had 24 cans and then I gave away 3 cans. How many cans are left?
   (D) I have 24 cans and my sister has 3 cans. How many cans do we have in total?

4. There are blue and orange marbles in a bag. The probability of randomly choosing an orange marble is 2 in 7. If there are 15 blue marbles in the bag, how many total marbles are there in the bag?

(A) 5
(B) 6
(C) 15
(D) 21

5. Use the given coordinate grid.

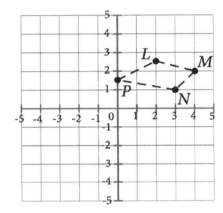

What are the coordinates of point *N*?

(A) $(4, 2)$
(B) $(3, 1)$
(C) $(2, 3)$
(D) $(0, 1.5)$

Workout #15 Answers

Vocabulary

Roots questions

1. The root *uni* means "one" and the root *form* means "shape", so *uniform* literally means "one shape". If items are *uniform*, then they would all be the same shape or identical to one another.

2. The root *ex* means "out", so *exclaim* literally means "to shout out".

Words to remember questions

1. A *morsel* of bread would probably not be satisfying. Just a little bit of bread would not be very filling.

2. If a person *obstructs justice*, it means that he or she gets in the way of justice being done. For example, if someone won't tell the police about a crime he or she witnessed, he or she is obstructing justice.

Verbal Reasoning practice

Synonym practice

1. D is the correct answer choice. *Hurl* is a word to remember from workout #13 so please review those words if you missed this question.

2. B is the correct answer choice. *Formless* has two roots – *form* that means "shape" and *less* which means "without" – so *formless* literally means "without shape", or shapeless.

3. D is the correct answer choice. *Clamor* has the *clam* root which means "to shout". Answer choice D comes closest to the meaning of this root.

4. B is the correct answer choice. *Hoist* is a word to remember from workout #12 so please review those words if you missed this question.

Sentence Completions practice

1. C is the correct answer choice. In this sentence, the word "that" tells us that the blank must refer back to something earlier in the sentence. Since the beginning of the sentence talks about "a tiny bit" we know that we are looking for a word that means a tiny bit, which *morsel* does. *Morsel* is also a word to remember from this workout so please review those words if you didn't know what *morsel* meant.

2. A is the correct answer choice. We are looking for a word that goes along with the word *safe* and a *haven* is a safe place. *Haven* is a word to remember from workout #14 so please review those words if you couldn't remember the meaning of the word *haven*.

3. C is the correct answer choice. The word *although* tells us that the second part of the sentence should change direction from the first part of the sentence. The first part of the sentence tells us that Marilyn Monroe was dismissed as a serious actress, so the second part of the sentence should tell us that she should be respected as a serious actress. Choice C does this.

Reading Comprehension practice

Reading passage practice

1. D is the correct answer choice. This is mainly a passage concerned with informing a reader about something, not presenting an argument (answer choices A and B) or persuading the reader (choice C).

2. B is the correct answer choice. The passage tells us, "its inhabitants wanted a way to spread the word that South Dakota had a great climate for running an agricultural business, such as farming." Answer choice B restates this idea.

3. C is the correct answer choice. This is a vocabulary in context question so we will cross out the word "inhabitants" in the passage and then plug in answer choices. If we do this, we find that the meaning of the sentence remains the same if we plug in the word *residents* where the word *inhabitants* was.

4. A is the correct answer. The passage tells us that 500,000 people visit the Corn Palace each year.

5. B is the correct answer choice. If we use ruling out, we can easily rule out choices A and C. The passage tells us that people still visit the Corn Palace and that it is large enough to host basketball tournaments. Now we have to decide if it is frequently changing or completely rebuilt every year. The passage tells us that the Corn Palace from 1921 is still in use but that the murals are changed out every year. This makes answer choice B the best choice.

Math practice

Quantitative Reasoning and Mathematics Achievement practice

1. C is the correct answer choice. This question is testing the order of operations, or PEMDAS. We need to do the calculation in parentheses first. If we do that we get $3 \times (4 + 6) = 3 \times (10) = 3 \times 10$.

2. A is the correct answer choice. If you missed this question, go back and make sure that you borrowed correctly. We perform this calculation just like any other subtraction problem only we need to remember to line up the decimal points so that we don't confuse place values.

3. B is the correct answer choice. Since the equation uses division, we are looking for a story that gives us the total and then asks for either the number of groups or the size of each group. Choice B gives us the total number of cans (24) and how many groups there are (3 rows) and then asks us to solve for how many are in each group (8), so it is the story that best fits the equation.

4. D is the correct answer choice. The key to this question is that we need to find the probability for the type of item that we are given the actual number for. If the probability of drawing an orange marble is 2 out of 7, then the probability of drawing a blue marble must be 5 out of 7. Now we can set up a proportion:

$$\frac{5 \text{ blue marbles}}{7 \text{ total marbles}} = \frac{15 \text{ blue marbles}}{t \text{ total marbles}}$$

Now let's use cross-multiplying to solve:

$5 \times t = 7 \times 15$
$5t = 105$
$t = 21$

There are a total of 21 marbles in the bag.

5. B is the correct answer choice. To answer this question, we have to remember to start at the origin (where the x and y axes cross), run, and then jump. This means that our first coordinate tells us how many spaces to go over on the x-axis and the second coordinate tells us how many spaces to go up. To get to point N, we would have to go over 3 spaces and then up 1 so N has the coordinates of $(3, 1)$.

Appendix A – Tips for the Essay

When you take the ISEE, you will be asked to complete an essay at the very end of the test. You will be given 30 minutes and two pages to write your response.

You will also be given a piece of paper to take notes on.

- Essay is at the end of the test
- 30 minutes to complete
- Two pages to write on, plus one piece of paper for notes

Your essay will NOT be scored. Rather, a copy of it will be sent to the schools that you apply to. This writing sample is a great way for the admissions committee to get to know you better.

- Let your personality shine through so that admissions officers can get to know you better

You will be given a question to write from. The questions are topics that you can relate to your own life.

Here are some examples that are like the questions that you will see on the ISEE:

1. If you could change one thing about your school, what would it be? Why would you want to change it?

2. Who is your favorite teacher? Why did you choose this teacher?

3. If school was suddenly cancelled for the day, what would you do with your day? Describe in detail.

   (There are more sample questions in ERB's official guide, *What to Expect on the ISEE*)

To approach the essay, follow this three-step plan

Step 1: Plan

- Take just a couple of minutes and plan, it will be time well spent
- Be sure to know what your main idea is and how each paragraph will be different
- Use the piece of paper provided

Step 2: Write

- Break your writing into paragraphs – don't do a two-page blob
- Write legibly – it does not have to be perfect and schools know that you are writing with a time limit, but if the admissions officers can't read what you wrote, they can't judge it
- Remember that each paragraph should have its own idea

Step 3: Edit/proofread

- Save a couple of minutes at the end to look over your work
- You won't be able to do a major editing job where you move around sentences and rewrite portions
- Look for where you may have left out a word or misspelled something
- Make your marks simple and clear – if you need to take something out, put a single line through it and use a carat to insert words that you forgot

The essay is not graded, but the schools that you apply to do receive a copy.

What are schools looking for?

Organization

There should be structure to your writing. You need to have an introduction, good details to back up your main point, and a conclusion. Each paragraph should have its own idea.

Word choice

Use descriptive language. Don't describe anything as "nice" or "good". Describe specifically why something is nice or good. Good writing shows us and DOESN'T tell us.

Creativity and development of ideas

It is not enough just to be able to fit your writing into the form that you were taught in school. These prompts are designed to show how you think. This is your chance to shine!

The essay is a place for you to showcase your writing skills. It is one more piece of information that the admissions committee will use in making their decisions.

The best way to get better at writing an essay is to practice. Try writing about one or more of the questions above. Use the prompts from *What to Expect on the ISEE*. Have a trusted adult help you analyze your writing sample and figure out how you can improve.

- Practice writing an essay before the actual test
- Have a teacher or parent help you analyze your practice essays

Looking for more instruction and practice?

Check out our other books for the Lower Level ISEE:

Success on the Lower Level ISEE: A Complete Course

- ✓ Strategies to use for each section of the Lower Level ISEE
- ✓ Reading and vocabulary drills
- ✓ In-depth math content instruction with practice sets
- ✓ 1 full-length practice test

The Best Unofficial Practice Tests for the Lower Level ISEE

- ✓ 2 full-length practice tests (different from the practice test in *Success on the Lower Level ISEE*)

Was *30 Days to Acing the Lower Level ISEE* helpful to you?
Please consider leaving a review with the merchant where you purchased the book.
We welcome your suggestions at *feedback@testprepworks.com*.

TEST PREP WORKS, LLC.

Books by Test Prep Works

	Content instruction	Test-taking strategies	Practice problems	Full-length practice tests
ISEE				
Lower Level (for students applying for admission to grades 5-6)				
Success on the Lower Level ISEE	✓	✓	✓	✓ (1)
30 Days to Acing the Lower Level ISEE		✓	✓	
The Best Unofficial Practice Tests for the Lower Level ISEE				✓ (2)
Middle Level (for students applying for admission to grades 7-8)				
Success on the Middle Level ISEE	✓	✓	✓	✓ (1)
The Best Unofficial Practice Tests for the Middle Level ISEE				✓ (2)
Upper Level (for students applying for admission to grades 9-12)				
Success on the Upper Level ISEE	✓	✓	✓	✓ (1)
The Best Unofficial Practice Tests for the Upper Level ISEE				✓ (2)
SSAT				
Middle Level (for students applying for admission to grades 6-8)				
Success on the Middle Level SSAT	✓	✓	✓	
The Best Unofficial Practice Tests for the Middle Level SSAT (coming soon)				✓ (2)
Upper Level (for students applying for admission to grades 9-12)				
Success on the Upper Level SSAT	✓	✓	✓	✓ (1)
30 Days to Acing the Upper Level SSAT		✓	✓	
The Best Unofficial Practice Tests for the Upper Level SSAT				✓ (2)

TEST PREP WORKS, LLC.

58101359R00123

Made in the USA
Lexington, KY
03 December 2016